English for Construction

1

Vocational English
Course Book

...endo
...onamy

Contents

1 The construction industry

- introduce yourself and others
- talk about jobs in the construction industry
- describe types of construction
- understand a house plan

Introductions

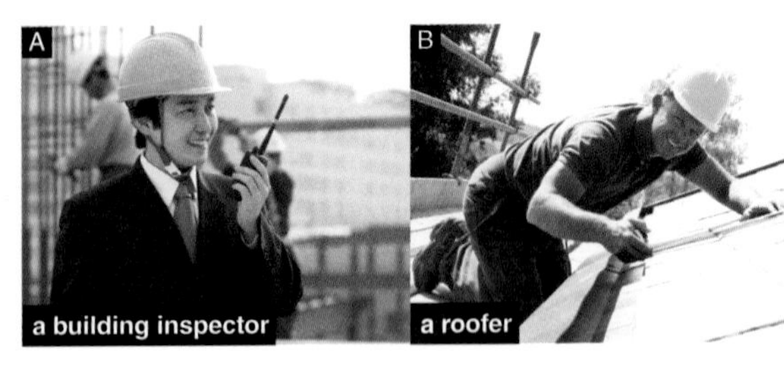

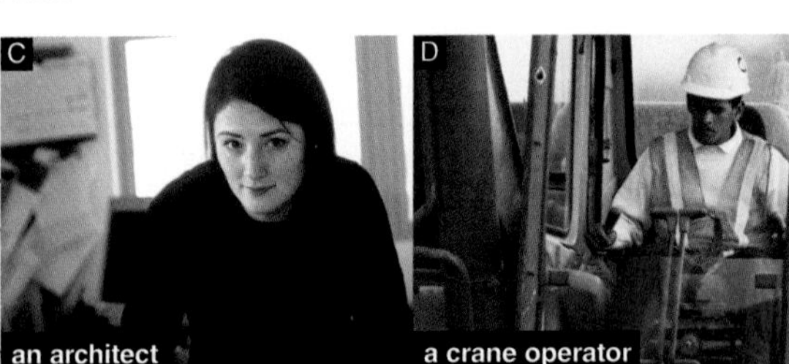

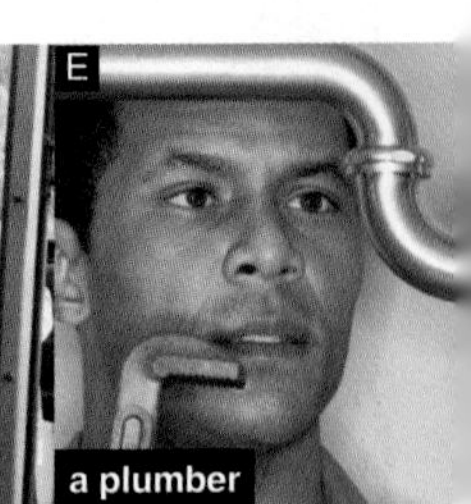

Vocabulary

1 Match photos A–E to texts 1–5.

1 Hello, I'm Kamal Boukhaled, from Morocco. I'm a plumber. ______
2 I'm Isabelle Roux, from France. I'm an architect. ______
3 Hi, my name's Santiago Cruz. I'm from Venezuela. I'm a crane operator. ______
4 Hi, I'm Karol Nowacki. I'm from Poland. I'm a roofer. ______
5 Hello there. My name's Jun Takahashi. I'm from Japan. I'm a building inspector. ______

Listening

2 ▶ 02 Complete these conversations. Then listen and compare your answers.

1 Jun: Hi! I'm Jun Takahashi, from the Ministry.
Isabelle: Hi, Mr Takahashi. (1) ______ Isabelle Roux. I'm from (2) ______ . I'm the architect on this project.
Jun: Ah, I'm a building (3) ______ .
Isabelle: Pleased to (4) ______ you.

2 Karol: Hi! Karol Nowacki.
Santiago: Santiago Cruz.
Karol: What do you do, Santiago?
Santiago: I'm a crane (5) ______ . And you?
Karol: Me? I'm a(n) (6) ______ .

3 Kamal: Hi! My (7) ______ is Kamal Boukhaled.
Santiago: Hi, Kamal. I'm Santiago.
Kamal: (8) ______ are you from?
Santiago: From Caracas, Venezuela.
Kamal: Ah, Caracas. A beautiful city. I come from (9) ______ .

4 Kamal: Hello. (10) ______ name's Kamal Boukhaled.
Karol: Hi, Kamal. I'm Karol Nowacki. And this is Isabelle Roux.
Kamal: Hello, Isabelle.
Isabelle: Pleased to meet you.
Karol: What do you (11) ______, Kamal?
Kamal: I'm a plumber.
Karol: I'm a roofer. And Isabelle designs buildings.
Kamal: She's a(n) (12) ______?
Isabelle: Yes, that's right.

Reading **3** Read this text and underline the verbs.

Harun Rashid is 35 years old. He comes from Alexandria, but lives and works in Cairo.

Harun is a general contractor. He hires subcontractors to work on building projects. He also organises the material and equipment. Harun has a lot of experience in the construction industry.

Harun always works hard. Sometimes he has meetings with clients. Sometimes he visits construction sites. And sometimes he deals with suppliers. He is always busy.

But Friday is different. Harun never works on Fridays. Friday is a day off.

4 Correct these sentences.

1 Harun Rashid is a plumber. ________
2 He hires clients to work on building projects. ________
3 He has a lot of experience in the tourist industry. ________
4 He never visits construction sites. ________
5 He always works on Fridays. ________

Language

Present simple: *be*

We use ***be*** to say who somebody is or what something is.	*I**'m** Santiago Cruz. He**'s** Harun Rashid.* *This **is** a construction site. We**'re** roofers.*
We use ***be*** to ask personal questions.	*What**'s** your name? My name**'s** Karol.*

Present simple: regular verbs

We use the **present simple** to talk about routines, permanent situations and general truths.	*We **work** in an office.* *Water **freezes** at 0°C.*
We use **adverbs of frequency** and **time expressions** with the present simple.	*Harun Rashid **never** works **on Fridays**.* *They work **every Saturday**.*

Speaking **5** Work in pairs and introduce yourselves. Use this model to help you.

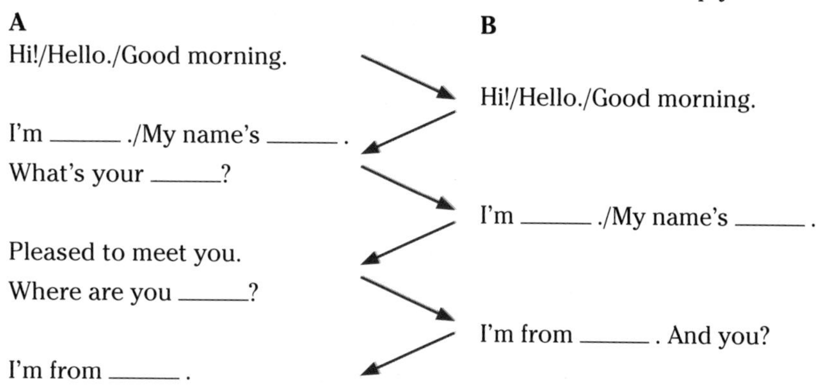

Finding out more

Listening

1 03 Listen and repeat the letters of the alphabet.

The alphabet
A, H, J, K
B, C, D, E, G, P, T, V, Z (American English)
F, L, M, N, S, X, Z (British English)
I, Y
O
Q, U, W
R

2 04 Listen and write the surnames you hear.

1 Robert ______
2 Carlos ______
3 Sasha ______

Speaking

3 Work in pairs. Student A look at the information on this page. Student B look at the information on page 68.

Student A

Read the letters to Student B. Write the letters Student B says. What do the letters mean?

HVAC rpm AC JCB

HVAC = heating, ventilation and air conditioning
rpm = revolutions per minute
AC = alternating current
JCB = JC Bamford Excavators Limited (a construction equipment manufacturer)

4 Practise this conversation with your classmates. Write the names.

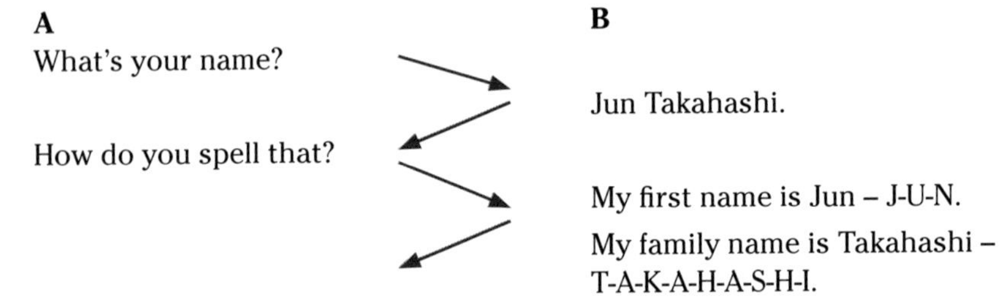

A	**B**
What's your name?	
	Jun Takahashi.
How do you spell that?	
	My first name is Jun – J-U-N. My family name is Takahashi – T-A-K-A-H-A-S-H-I.
Thank you.	

Listening **5** 05 Listen to three conversations. Write the jobs you hear for each person 1–8.

1 Ahmed: ________
2 Tariq: ________
3 Jacek: ________
4 Luis: ________
5 Rob: ________
6 Pierre: ________
7 Kim: ________
8 Antonio: ________

Language

Wh- questions

Wh- questions begin with a question word (e.g. *What*, *Where*, *How*).

We use ***what*** when we want to know about something.	***What***'s *your name?* ***What*** *do you do?*
We use ***where*** to ask about places.	***Where*** *do you work?*
We use ***how*** to ask about the way to do something.	***How*** *do you spell that?*

Questions with *be*

We reverse the order of the verb *be* to form a question.	***He is*** *on site today.* → ***Is he*** *on site today?*

6 Read the three conversations in audio script 5 on page 72 and underline the questions in the conversations.

7 Complete these sentences with *What*, *Where* or *How*.

1 ______ do you live?
2 ______ do you do?
3 ______ are you?
4 ______'s your address?
5 ______ time is it?
6 ______ old are you?
7 ______ is the site?
8 ______ are you from?

8 Put the words in 1–6 in the correct order to make questions. Then match the questions to answers a–f.

1 ☐ what / he / do / does / ?
2 ☐ can / you / help / I / ?
3 ☐ how / spell / you / that / do / ?
4 ☐ where / work / you / do / ?
5 ☐ what / you / do / do / ?
6 ☐ are / the / manager / site / you / ?

a) He's a crane operator.
b) I'm a plumber.
c) On a building site.
d) C-H-E-S-T-E-R-T-O-N-S.
e) I'm looking for Kim.
f) Yes, I am.

Speaking **9** Work in pairs. Take turns to ask and answer questions about the people in 5.

A	**B**
What does Kim do? →	
	She's a site manager.
What about Tariq? ← →	
	Tariq is a … .
OK. Your turn. ←	

The construction industry

Listening **1** 06 Listen and write the missing letters.

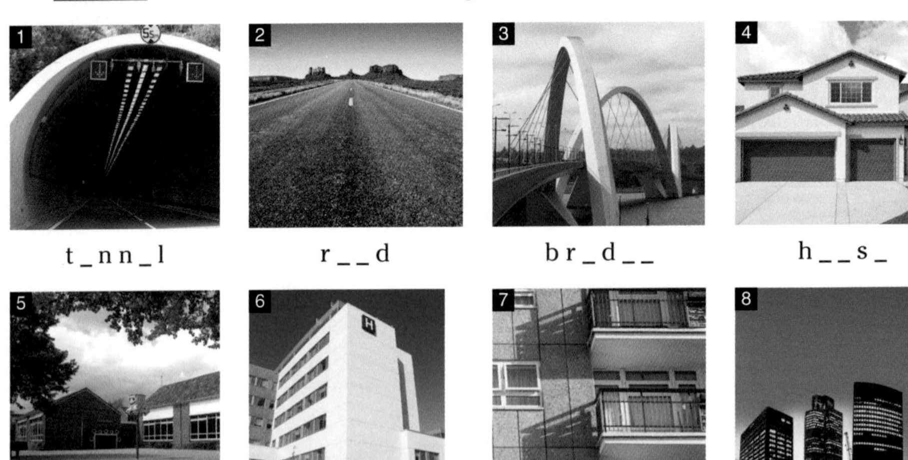

1 t _ n n _ l
2 r _ _ d
3 b r _ d _ _
4 h _ _ s _
5 s _ h _ _ l
6 _ o s p _ t _ l
7 a _ a _ t m _ _ t
8 o _ f i c _ b _ o _ k

2 07 Listen and write the types of construction you hear.

1 ________
2 ________
3 ________
4 ________
5 ________
6 ________

Speaking **3** Choose a role card. Introduce yourself to other students. Use the model below to help you.

1
Name: Kasia Katolsky
Job: building inspector
Typical projects: factories, schools
From: Katowice, Poland

2
Name: Thomas Smith
Job: roofer
Typical projects: residential projects (houses, apartments)
From: Toronto, Canada

3
Name: Mohamed bin Ali
Job: site manager
Typical projects: hospitals
From: Dubai, United Arab Emirates (UAE)

4
Name: Park Ji-Wung
Job: crane operator
Typical projects: bridges, flyovers
From: Seoul, Korea

A	B
Hi! I'm ________ ./ My name's ________ .	
	Hi! I'm Raja Anand./My name's Raja Anand.
What do you do?	
	I'm a general contractor.
What types of construction do you work on?	
	We build apartment blocks.
Where are you from?	
	I'm from Mumbai, India.

Reading **4** Read this text and complete charts A and B.

The construction industry in the UK consists of four different sectors. The residential sector deals with houses and apartments. The industrial sector deals with big projects like factories and power plants. The infrastructure sector is for projects like roads, bridges and tunnels. The commercial sector is for things like schools, hospitals and office blocks. The client pays for the project and hires general contractors to deal with subcontractors, equipment and materials.

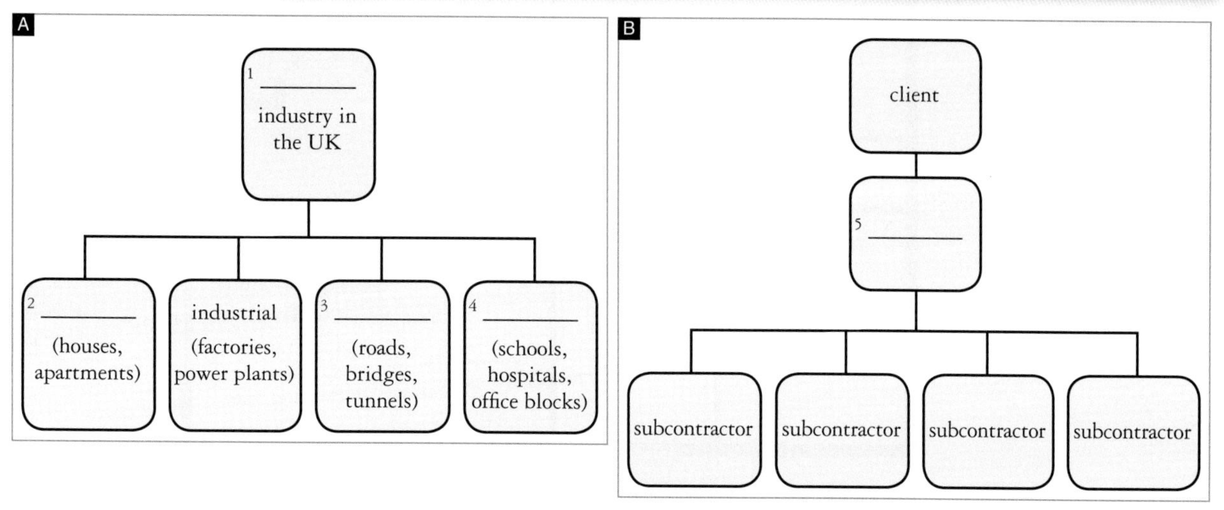

Vocabulary **5** Work in pairs. Take turns to draw different types of construction and say what they are.

6 Complete these sentences with the verbs in the box.

are	consists of	deal with	hires	pays for

1 The general contractor ________ subcontractors.
2 General contractors ________ subcontractors, equipment and materials.
3 The team ________ a site manager, three roofers and a plumber.
4 Roads, bridges and tunnels ________ infrastructure sector projects.
5 The client ________ the project.

Language

Plurals

We add **-s**, **-es**, or **-ies** to make a noun **plural**.	*apartment → apartment**s*** *box → box**es*** *factory → factor**ies***

7 Read the text in 4 again and underline the plurals.

Speaking **8** Work in groups. Think about the construction industry in your area. List examples of the following.

1 clients
2 general contractors
3 subcontractors
4 residential sector projects
5 infrastructure sector projects
6 commercial sector projects
7 industrial sector projects

Parts of a house

Listening 1 08 Look at house plans A and B. Then listen. Does the speaker describe the house correctly?

first floor (American English) = ground floor (British English)

A

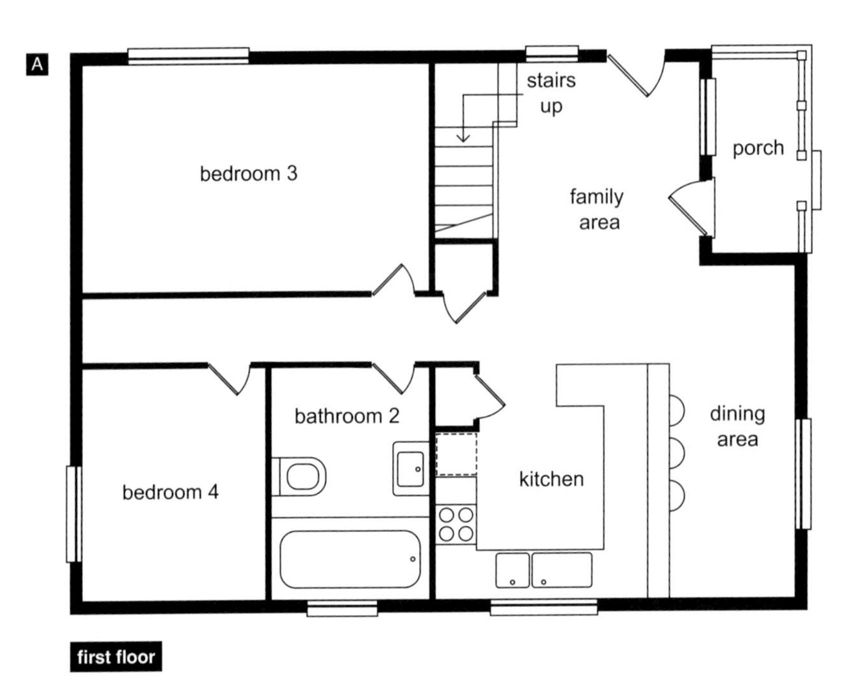

B

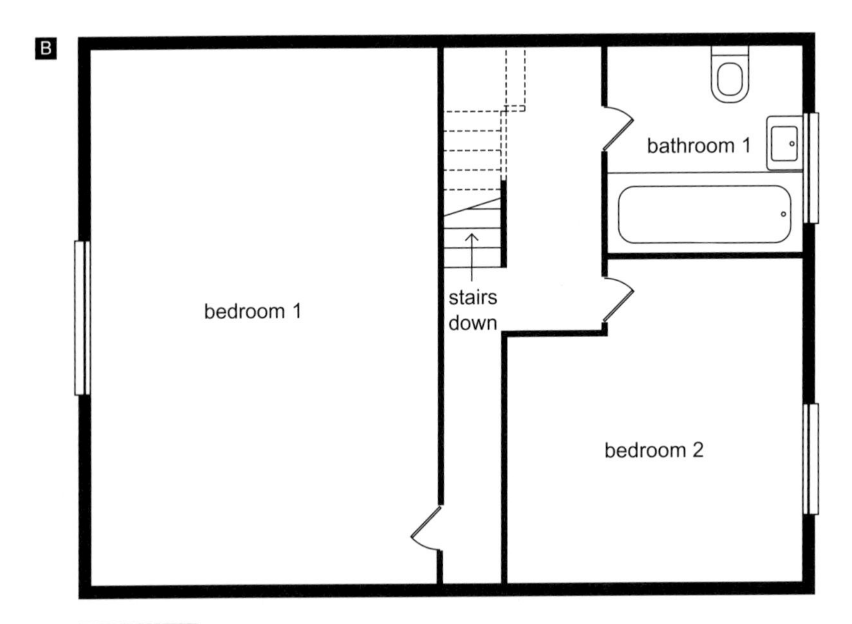

Speaking 2 Work in pairs. Draw a simple house plan and label it. Show it to your partner and ask and answer questions about it. Then repeat with a new partner.

A: *What's this?*
B: *This is a bathroom.*
A: *And this?*
B: *This is the first floor. And this is the second floor.*

Review

Writing

1 Complete these sentences with information about yourself.

1 My name's … .
2 I'm an … .
3 I live in … .
4 I come from … .

2 Match these questions to your answers in 1.

a) Where are you from?
b) What do you do?
c) What's your name?
d) Where do you live?

3 Write four things a general contractor does. Use the correct form of the verbs in the box.

deal with hire organise visit

4 Write four things you do in your job. If you don't work, choose a job from the unit.

Vocabulary

5 Complete these sentences.

1 The ________ industry consists of four sectors.
2 The ________ sector deals with houses and apartments.
3 The ________ sector deals with roads, bridges and tunnels.
4 The ________ sector deals with schools, hospitals and office blocks.
5 The ________ sector deals with factories and power plants.

6 Write five examples of the following.

1 jobs in the construction industry
2 types of construction
3 parts of a house

7 Complete this text with the words and phrases in the box.

about a project a new office block architect residential area subcontractor supplier

Today I have three meetings. First, I have a meeting (1) ________ with a client and a(n) (2) ________ in Bulaq. The project is an apartment block in a(n) (3) ________ . I have a lot of experience with apartment blocks, but not in this part of Cairo. After lunch, I have a meeting with a new (4) ________ on a construction site in Al Nasr Road. This meeting is about labourers and equipment for (5) ________ . In the evening, I have a meeting with a(n) (6) ________ to discuss materials for a construction site in Tura. It's a busy day as always!

8 What do the following letters mean?

1 HVAC ________
2 AC ________
3 PPE ________
4 HV ________
5 kg ________
6 POL ________
7 cm ________
8 rpm ________

2 Trades

- describe trades and the stages of trade train
- talk about trade materials
- give and understand instructions for erectin scaffolding
- give personal information

Trades and training

Vocabulary **1** Label tradespeople 1–8 with the words in the box.

> carpenter concrete finisher electrician glazier painter
> plumber roofer welder

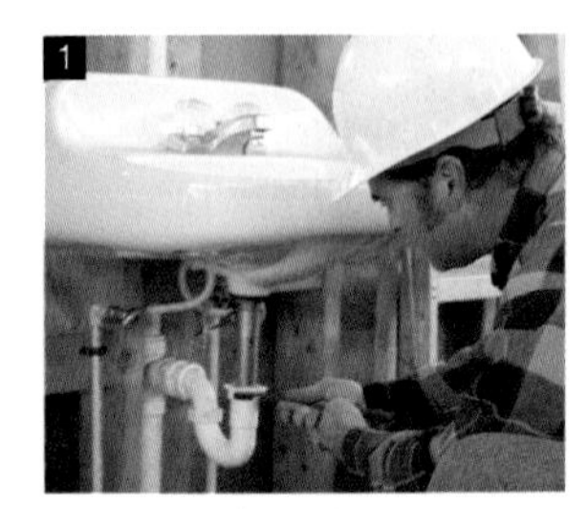

a p ________

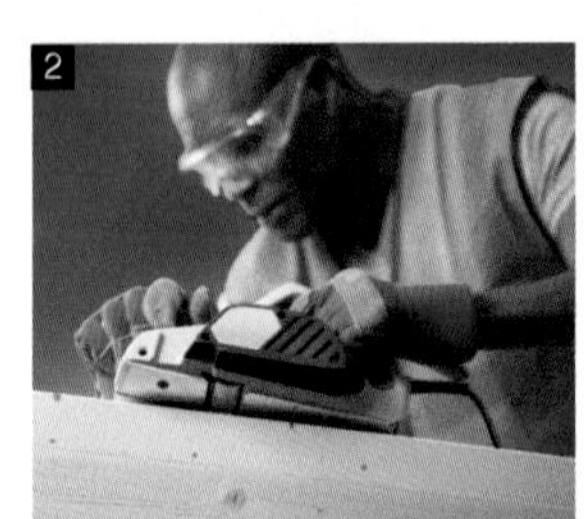

a c ________

a c ________ f ________

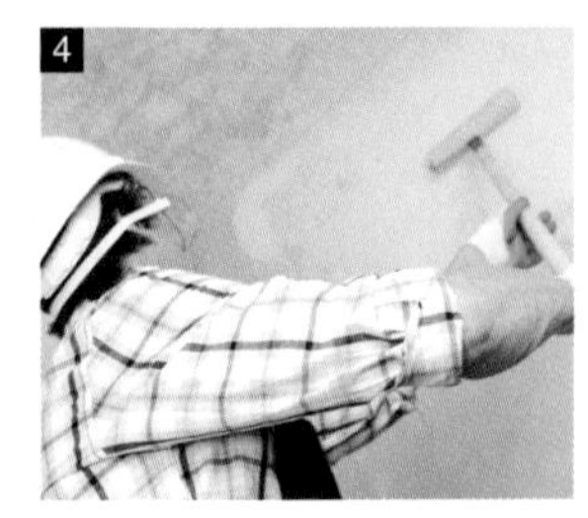

a p ________

a r ________

a w ________

a g ________

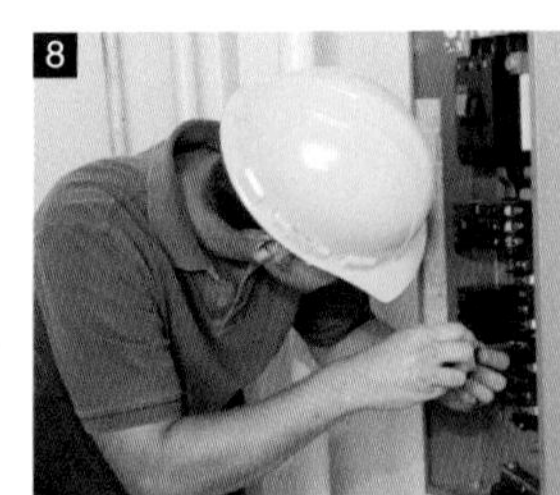

an e ________

Reading **2** Read this text and underline the trades. Use the photos in 1 to help you.

You can refer to tradespeople in several ways:
- tradesperson/ tradespeople (for men and women)
- tradesman/ tradesmen (for men)
- tradeswoman/ tradeswomen (for women)

A job in the construction industry?

The construction industry has different trades or 'crafts'. A tradesperson is a specialist and normally has a qualification from a vocational school or other training institute. Plumbers, electricians and roofers are all tradespeople. Other tradespeople on residential housing projects include carpenters, painters and concrete finishers. Tradespeople are often subcontractors and work for a general contractor or a client.

Vocabulary **3** Write the plurals for 1–5.

1 trade ________
2 craft ________
3 tradesman ________
4 housing project ________
5 general contractor ________

Listening **4** [09] Listen to Sam Smith talking about trades and complete these sentences.

Stage 1: *apprentice* He/She is (1) __________ at work.
Stage 2: *journeyman* He/She works (2) __________ .
Stage 3: *master* He/She supervises (3) __________ workers.

5 Listen again and answer these questions.

1 What is Sam Smith's trade? 2 Where does he work?

Vocabulary **6** Look at this list of courses at a vocational school. Match A–C to three of the courses. Then write the trade that each course refers to.

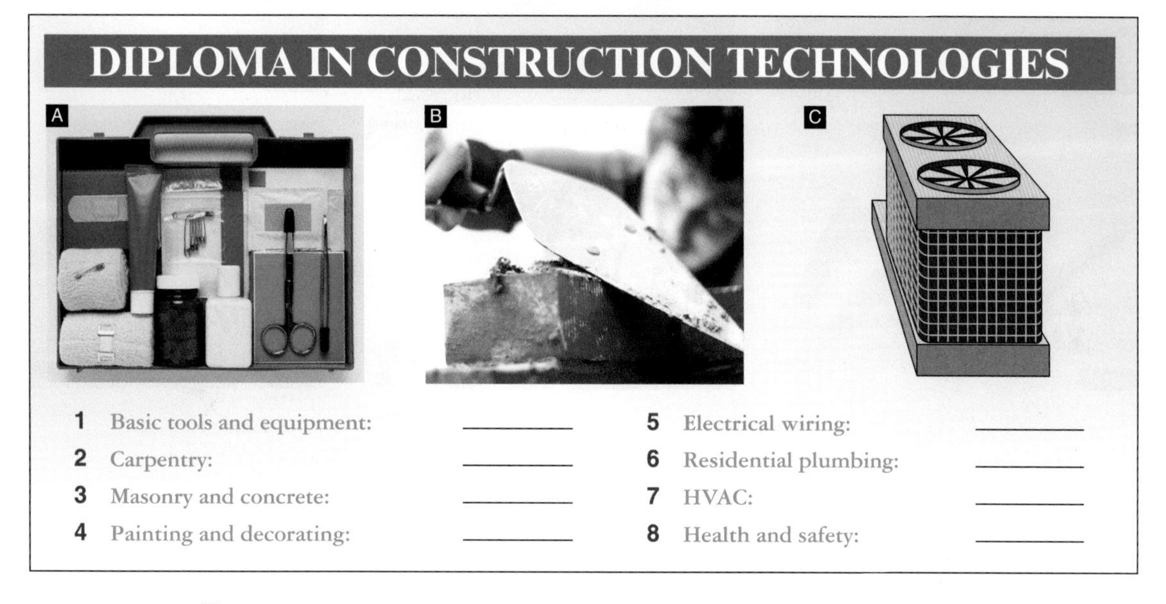

DIPLOMA IN CONSTRUCTION TECHNOLOGIES
A
B
C
1 Basic tools and equipment: __________
2 Carpentry: __________
3 Masonry and concrete: __________
4 Painting and decorating: __________
5 Electrical wiring: __________
6 Residential plumbing: __________
7 HVAC: __________
8 Health and safety: __________

Speaking **7** Work in pairs. Student A look at the information on this page. Student B look at the information on page 68.

Student A

Read this email from a vocational school in Calgary, Canada and underline the key information.

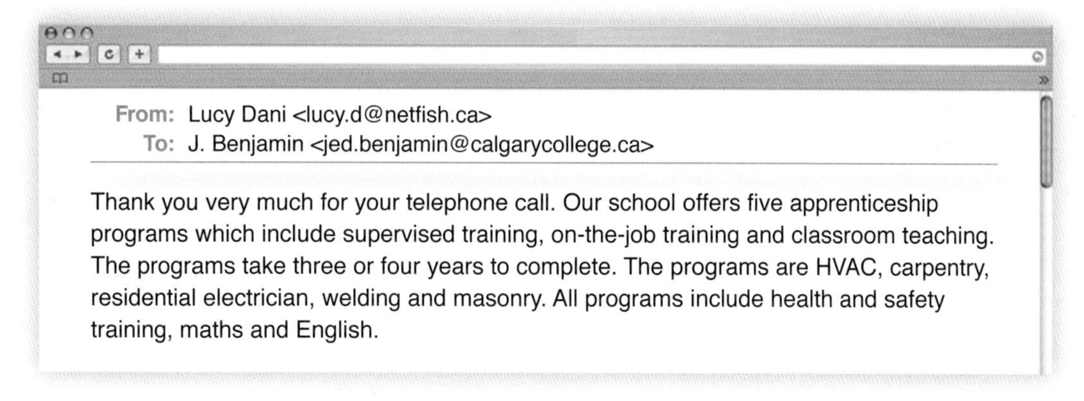

From: Lucy Dani <lucy.d@netfish.ca>
To: J. Benjamin <jed.benjamin@calgarycollege.ca>

Thank you very much for your telephone call. Our school offers five apprenticeship programs which include supervised training, on-the-job training and classroom teaching. The programs take three or four years to complete. The programs are HVAC, carpentry, residential electrician, welding and masonry. All programs include health and safety training, maths and English.

8 Work in the same pairs. Compare the two training institutes in 7. What things are the same? What things are different?

Trade materials

Vocabulary **1** What materials do these tradespeople use? Match materials A–F to tradespeople 1–6.

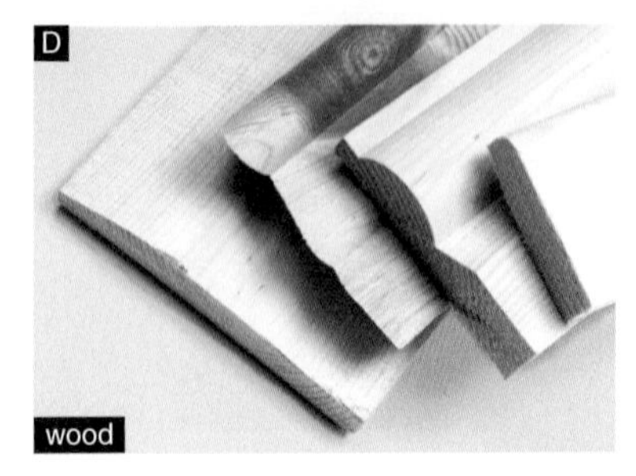

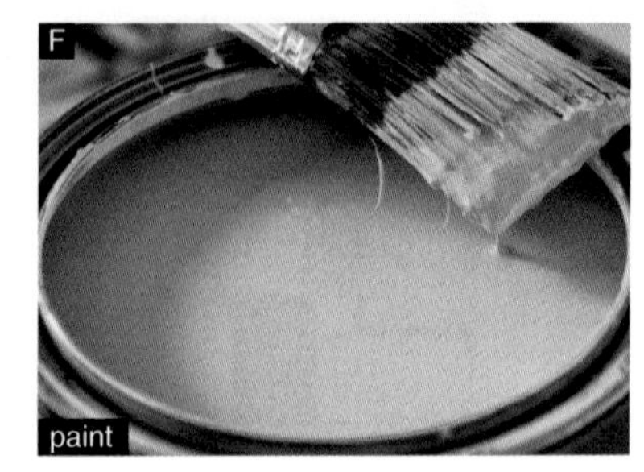

1 carpenter ______
2 glazier ______
3 painter ______
4 bricklayer and mason ______
5 welder ______
6 concrete finisher ______

2 Complete these sentences. Write one word in each gap.

1 I'm a bricklayer. I lay ________ .
2 I'm a(n) ________ . I do the wiring.
3 I'm a(n) ________ technician. I do the heating, ventilation and air conditioning.
4 I'm a carpenter. I work with ________ .
5 I'm a(n) ________ . I install windows.
6 I'm a painter. I use ________ to decorate houses.
7 I'm a welder. I weld ________ .

3 Complete this table with the missing verbs.

Nouns	Verbs
painter	(1) ________
decorator	(2) ________
instructor	(3) ________
welder	(4) ________
worker	(5) ________
supervisor	(6) ________
trainer	(7) ________

Speaking **4** Work in pairs. Ask your partner about things in the room.

A
What's that?

What's it made of?

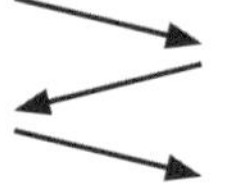

B
It's a window.

Glass and wood.

Language

Numbers 1–100

1	one	11	eleven	21	twenty-one
2	two	12	twelve	30	thirty
3	three	13	thirteen	40	forty
4	four	14	fourteen	50	fifty
5	five	15	fifteen	60	sixty
6	six	16	sixteen	70	seventy
7	seven	17	seventeen	80	eighty
8	eight	18	eighteen	90	ninety
9	nine	19	nineteen	100	a hundred/one hundred
10	ten	20	twenty		

5 10 Listen and tick ✓ the word you hear.

1 thirteen ☐ / thirty ☐
2 fourteen ☐ / forty ☐
3 sixteen ☐ / sixty ☐
4 nine ☐ / ninety ☐

6 11 Say these numbers. Then listen and check your answers.

1	56	34	89	63	76	21
2	13	30	14	40	16	60

7 Write these numbers.

1 twenty-four ________
2 thirty-three ________
3 forty-seven ________
4 sixty-nine ________
5 seventy-two ________
6 ninety-one ________

Listening

8 12 Listen to an architect talking about an office block. What do the numbers refer to? Match 1–5 to a–e.

1 six
2 22
3 44
4 32
5 two

a) number of windows per floor
b) number of floors
c) m^2
d) number of rooms per floor
e) windows per room

+	plus
–	minus
x	times
/	divided by
=	equals
( )	brackets

9 Make the calculations for the office block in 8.

Example: *1 264 (2 windows per room × 22 rooms = 44 windows; 44 windows × 6 floors = 264 windows)*

1 the total number of windows: 264
2 the total number of doors: ________
3 the total number of rooms: ________
4 the total space per floor (m^2): ________

Speaking

10 Write a number from 1 to 100 on a piece of paper. On the other side, write a calculation for the number.

11 Work in small groups. Read your calculation in 10 to the other students. The first student to answer correctly is the winner.

A: *Eight times eight, plus thirty-one, divided by five, plus thirty-eight equals ….*
B: *Fifty-eight.*
A: *Wrong!*
C: *Fifty-seven.*
A: *Correct!*

Instructions

Vocabulary **1** Match diagrams A–H to the verbs in the box.

adjust attach fill in fit join level nail slide onto

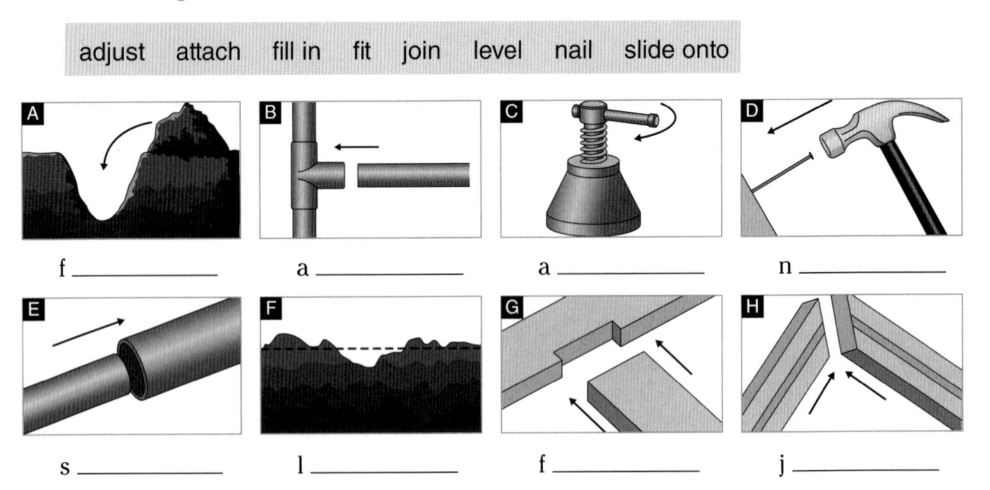

2 Look at these diagrams of scaffolding and complete the apprentice's notes. Then underline the verbs in the notes.

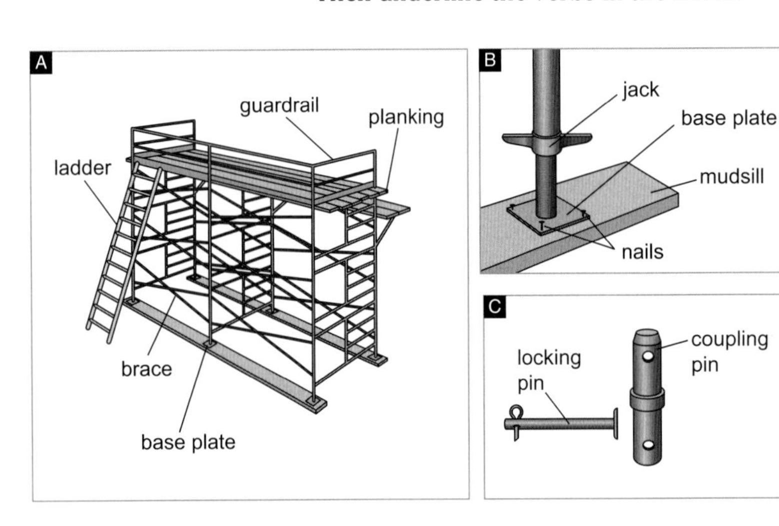

Erecting scaffolding

Fill in the holes and level the area. Nail the (1) ________ plates to the mudsills. Slide the frames onto the jacks. Adjust the jacks. Use (2) ________ pins and locking pins to join the frames. Attach t braces.

Fit the planking. Attach the guardrails. Attach the ladder. Inspect the scaffoldi

Remember!

Don't climb the scaffolding. Use the (3) ________ . Don't use bricks to lev the frames. Use the (4) ________ . Don't forget to use locking (5) ________ .

Language

The imperative

We can use the **imperative** to give instructions. Use ***don't*** (***do not***) before the verb to give negative instructions.	***Fill in*** *the holes.* ***Don't climb*** *the scaffolding.*
We can use the present simple instead of the imperative for informal instructions.	***You level*** *the frames.*

Sequencers

We can use ***first***, ***next***, ***then***, ***after that***, etc. to describe the order of instructions.	***First****, fill in the holes.* ***Next****, adjust the jacks.* ***Then****, fit the planking.*

Writing **3** Work in pairs. Close your books. Write instructions for erecting scaffolding.

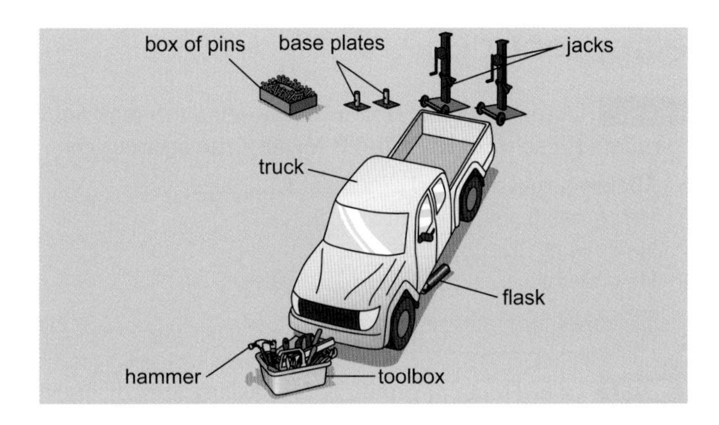

Listening **4** 13 Look at the illustration above. Then listen and complete these sentences.

1 The base plates are ________ the truck.
2 The hammer is ________ the toolbox, ________ the truck.
3 The coupling pins and locking pins are ________ a box, ________ the truck, ________ the base plates.
4 The jacks are ________ the truck.
5 The foreman's flask is ________ the truck.

Which sentence in the listening is incorrect?

Vocabulary **5** Listen again. Are these sentences *true* (T) or *false* (F)?

1 The base plates are next to the flask. (T / F)
2 The flask is in the truck. (T / F)
3 The jacks are behind the truck. (T / F)
4 The hammer is under the truck. (T / F)
5 The toolbox is in front of the truck. (T / F)

Language

Prepositions of place

We use **prepositions of place** to say where something is.

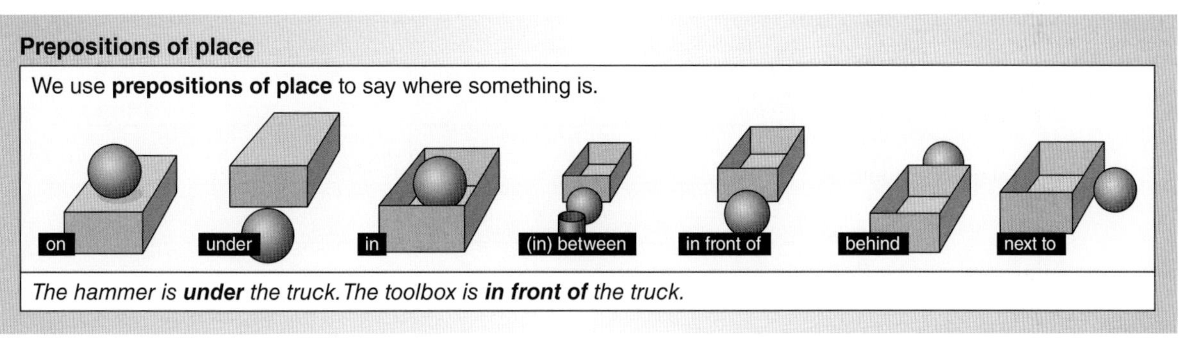

The hammer is ***under*** *the truck. The toolbox is* ***in front of*** *the truck.*

Writing **6** Write four sentences to show where the objects are in this illustration.

The apprentice

Listening **1** ▶ 14 Listen to a conversation between a foreman and an apprentice and complete these sentences about Mickey, the apprentice.

1 Mickey's real name is ________________ .
2 He comes from ________________ .
3 He lives in ________________ .
4 He goes to ________________ college.
5 He's a(n) ________________ .
6 He's ________________ years old.

2 ▶ 15 Listen to an apprentice, Jeff, asking Mickey questions about his birthday party and complete this information.

1 When: ________
2 Where: ________
3 Mickey's telephone number: ________

Language **3** Match questions 1–7 to answers a–g.

1 How old are you?	a) Yes, please.
2 What's your name?	b) It's 265775.
3 Where do you live?	c) It's seven o'clock.
4 Coffee?	d) I'm 33.
5 What's your telephone number?	e) It's John Smith.
6 How tall are you?	f) In Paris.
7 What time is it?	g) I'm 1.78 m.

4 Complete this form with information about yourself.

Name:	(1) ________________
Surname:	(2) ________________
Nickname:	(3) ________________
Address:	(4) ________________
Telephone number:	(5) ________________
Age:	(6) ________________
Height (in cm):	(7) ________________

Speaking **5** Work in pairs. Practise this conversation.

A: What's your telephone number?
B: It's ________ . And yours?
A: It's ________ .
A: How old are you?
B: I'm ________ . And you?
A: I'm ________ .
A: Where do you live?
B: In/At ________ . And you?
A: I live in/at ________ .

Review

Writing **1** Write the tradesperson that works with each of these materials.

1 wood	________	4 bricks	________
2 metal	________	5 concrete	________
3 glass	________	6 paint	________

2 Are these sentences *true* (T) or *false* (F)?

1 Journeymen work unsupervised. (T / F)
2 HVAC stands for 'heating, ventilation and air conditioning'. (T / F)
3 Twelve divided by three is three. (T / F)

3 Label these diagrams.

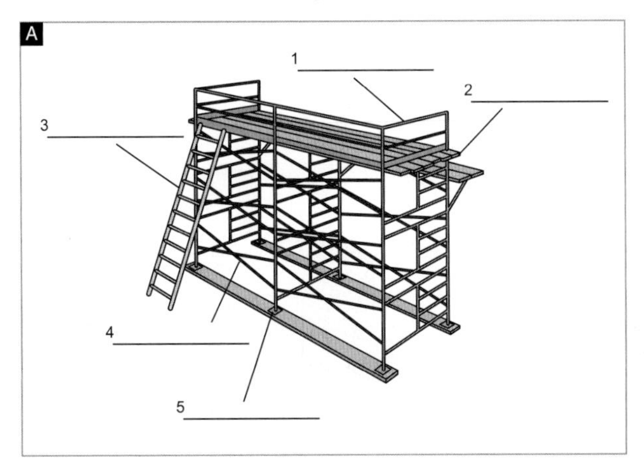

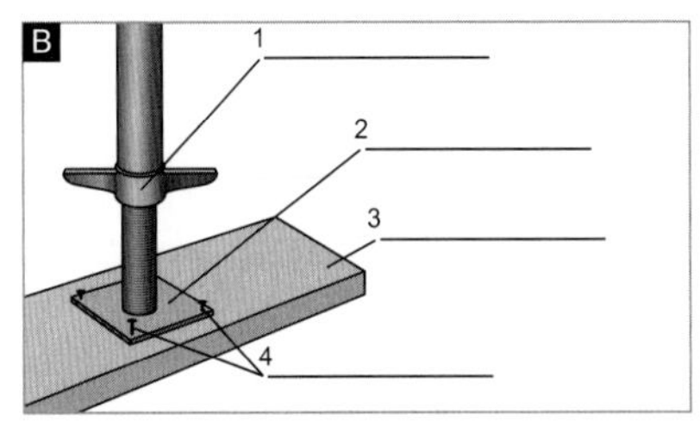

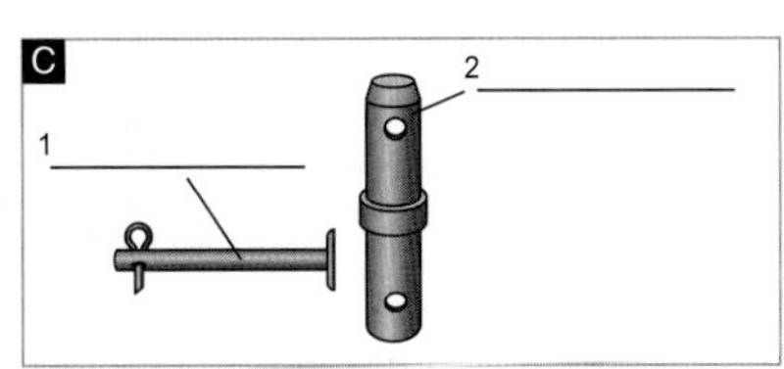

4 Write instructions for erecting scaffolding. Use the words in the box.

adjust attach fill in fit inspect join level nail slide use

5 Label these diagrams with the correct prepositions.

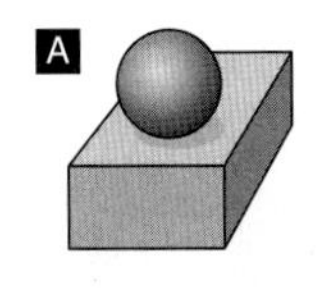

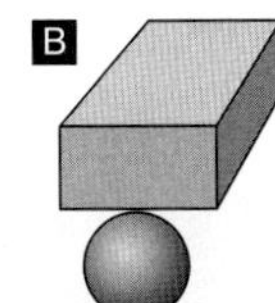

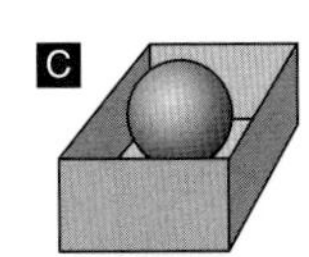

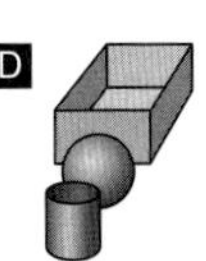

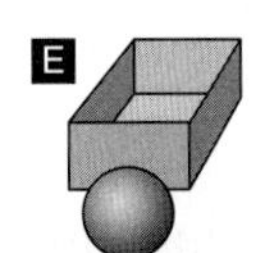

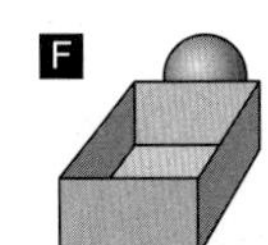

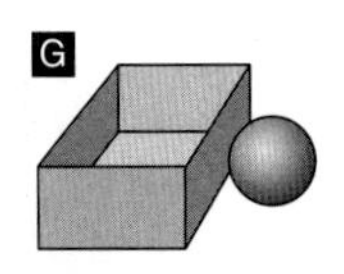

________ ________ ________ ________ ________ ________ ________

6 Complete this text with the words in the box.

apprentice(s) between on-the-job qualification safety years

The Institute of Masonry is in the centre of town, in (1) ________ a factory and an office block. It has 28 (2) ________ and three instructors. All the work is supervised and includes (3) ________ training, instruction on the use of modern equipment, tools and materials, and instruction on health and (4) ________ . The training takes three (5) ________ to complete. At the end of the course, apprentices get the Level 2 Diploma in Stone Masonry (6) ________ .

3 Heavy equipment

- talk about the delivery of heavy equipme
- describe how a crane and control units w
- give instructions for operating equipmen
- talk about mixing cement
- make conversation on site

Delivery

Vocabulary

1 Match sentences 1–4 to illustrations A–D. Then put sentences 1–4 in the correct order for unloading the crates.

1 ______ He's parking the truck on the hard standing. [1]
2 ______ He's unloading the crates. [ ]
3 ______ He's adjusting the stabiliser. [ ]
4 ______ He's attaching the slings to the hook. [ ]

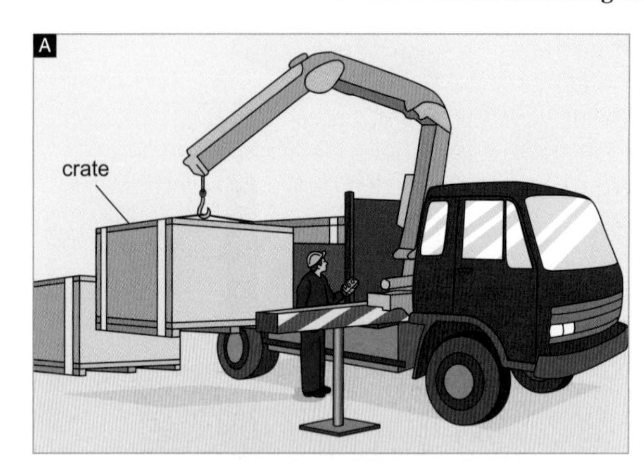

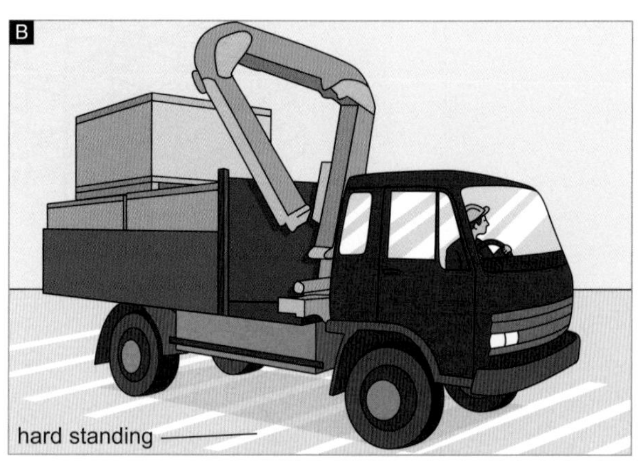

Listening

2 16 Listen to three conversations about deliveries and answer these questions.

1 What's in the crate?
2 What's in the box?
3 What's on the pallet?

3 17 Listen to three more conversations about deliveries and write the problem(s) with the following.

1 rebar 2 timber 3 sand

Language

Present continuous

We use the **present continuous** to talk about things that are happening now. We use the form ***am/is/are*** + ***-ing***.	***I am*** *phon**ing** the suppliers.* ***She is*** *wait**ing** for the timber.* ***We are*** *wait**ing** for the driver.*

4 Complete these sentences with the present continuous form of the verbs in brackets.

1 We ________ (unload) the truck.
2 I ________ (look for) the site manager.
3 He ________ (deliver) the sand.
4 She ________ (phone) the supplier.
5 They ________ (have) a meeting.
6 I'm sorry, but I ________ (run) late.

Vocabulary **5** A crane driver is describing to an apprentice how to operate a crane. Look at A–C and complete this text.

There are two levers. First, the lever on the left. Push it away from you to (1) ________ the load. Pull it towards you to (2) ________ it. OK? Second, the lever on the right. This moves the load (3) ________ or right. To move the load to the left, pull it (4) ________ you. To move the load to the right, push it (5) ________ from you. Any questions?

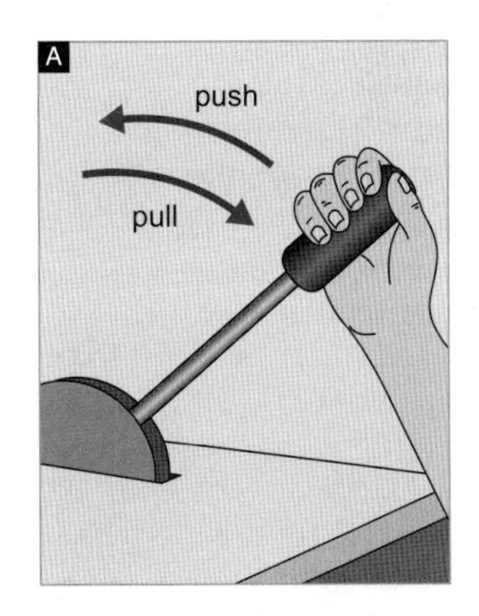

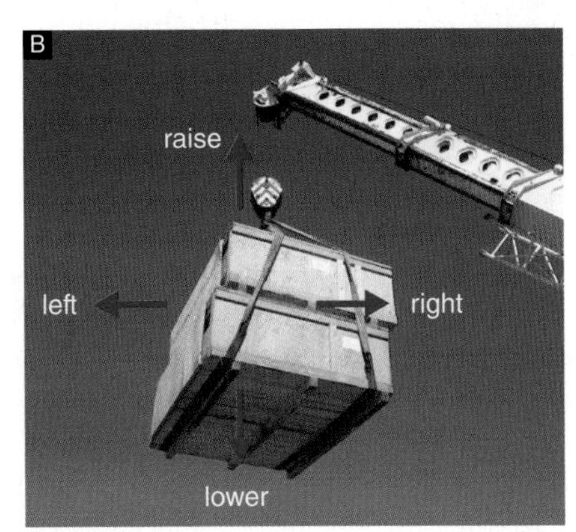

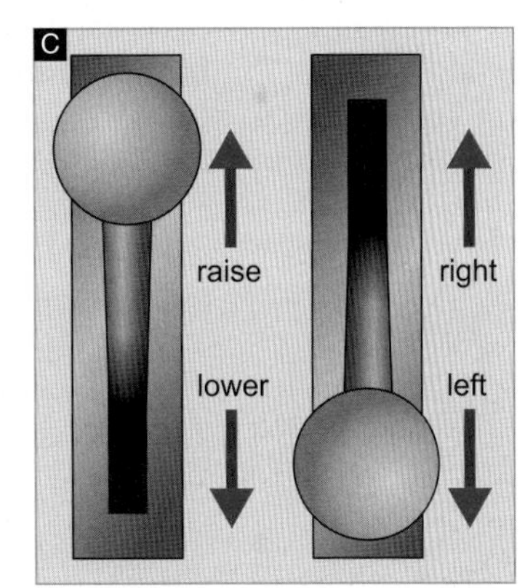

6 Answer the apprentice's questions.

1 How do I raise the load?
2 How do I lower the load?
3 How do I move the load to the left?
4 How do I move the load to the right?
5 How do I raise the load and move it to the right?
6 How do I lower the load and move it to the left?

Speaking **7** Work in pairs. Imagine you have two crane levers. Take turns to move them. Your partner says what you're doing with the load.

Cranes

Vocabulary **1** Look at the photos of the two cranes and complete this conversation.

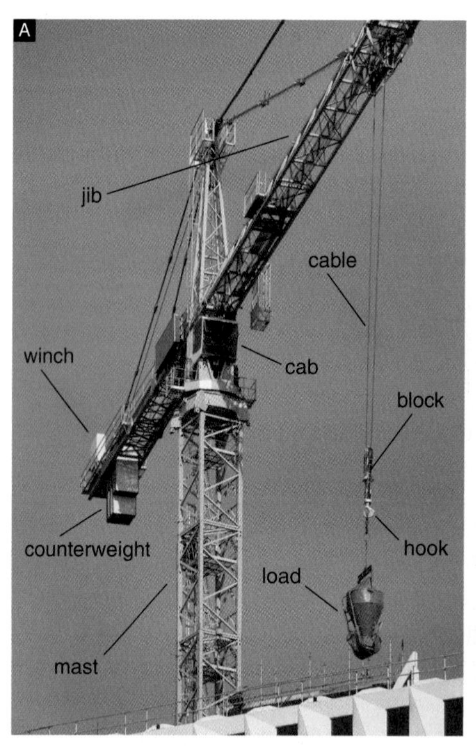

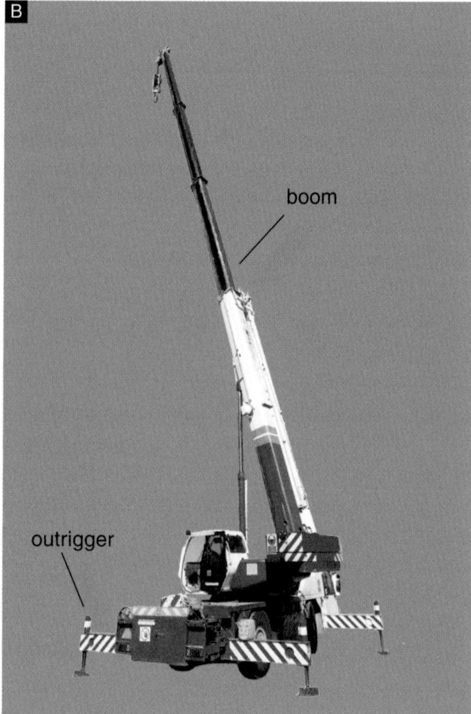

A: What are the differences between the two cranes?

B: The crane on the left is a tower crane. The operator sits in a(n) (1) ________ near the top of the (2) ________ . There's a counterweight behind the cab. The load is on the other side of the jib. The operator uses the winch and block to lower or raise the (3) ________ .

A: I see.

B: The crane on the right is a mobile crane. The operator's cab is near the ground. The operator extends or retracts the (4) ________, or moves it from left to right or up and down. Both cranes use stabilisers or (5) '________' and counterweights to maintain stability.

A: OK. Thank you.

2 Write the opposites.

1 extend ________
2 lower ________
3 left ________

3 Match 1–5 to a–e to make expressions about cranes.

1 operator's	a) crane
2 extend	b) cab
3 mobile	c) the boom
4 raise	d) the load
5 tower	e) crane

4 Work in pairs. Close your books. Student A draw a tower crane for Student B to label. Student B draw a mobile crane for Student A to label. Check each other's work.

Listening **5** 18 Listen to a description of crane controls and look at A and B. Then complete this text.

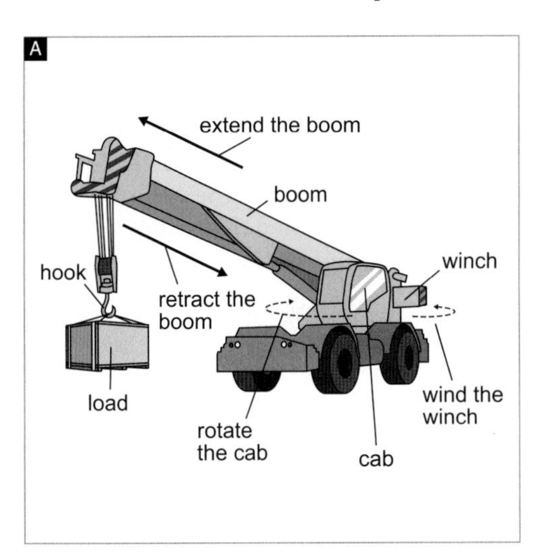

Crane operators use different controls to raise and lower the (1) ________, rotate the cab, extend and retract the boom, wind and unwind the (2) ________ and control other equipment. This operator has two (3) ________ . One controls left-to-right movement of the boom and the other controls forward and backward movement. The operator uses the foot (4) ________ to retract or extend the boom.

B

joystick

foot pedal

6 Listen again and check your answers to 5.

Language

There is/There are

We use ***there is/there are*** to say that somebody or something exists.	***There is*** *a key switch on the right.* ***There are*** *two joysticks.*
Singular questions:	***Is there*** *a start button? Yes,* ***there is****./No,* ***there isn't****.*
Plural questions:	***Are there*** *any buttons? Yes,* ***there are****./No,* ***there aren't****.*
Negative forms:	***There isn't*** *a light.* (singular) ***There aren't*** *any switches.* (plural)

Reading **7** Read this text about a remote control and label the illustration.

Sometimes crane operators use remote controls. In this model there's a stop button on the left. There's a key switch on the right. There are two joysticks in the middle. There are three toggle switches on the top.

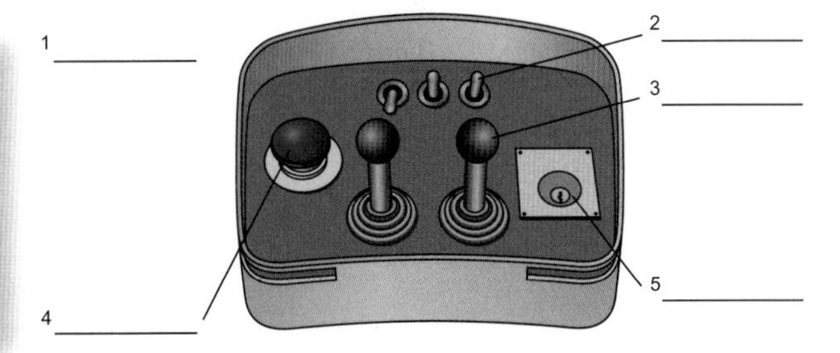

Writing **8** Rewrite the text in 7 for this remote control.

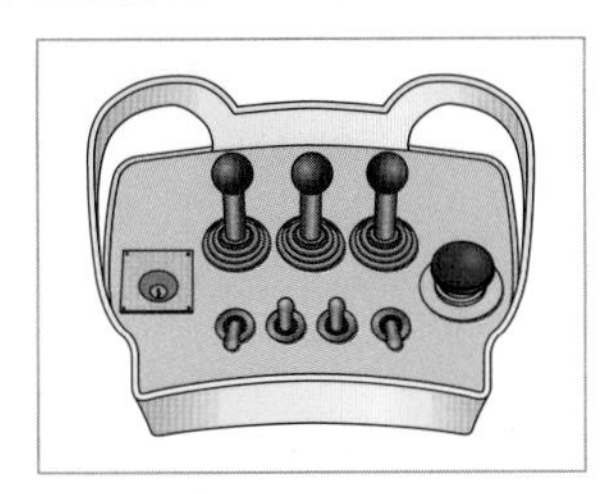

Speaking **9** Work in pairs. Draw a remote control. Put the controls where you like. Describe it for your partner to draw.

Controls and equipment

Listening **1** ▶ 19 Match questions 1–6 to answers a–f. Then listen and check your answers.

1 What's this? A remote control?
2 What's this for?
3 What does this do?
4 How do I extend the boom?
5 How do I lower the boom?
6 What's this switch for? Is it the power switch?

a) Lower it? You move the joystick.
b) It's a remote control. That's right.
c) Yes, that's the power switch.
d) Extend it? You use the pedal.
e) It's for extending the boom.
f) It starts the motor.

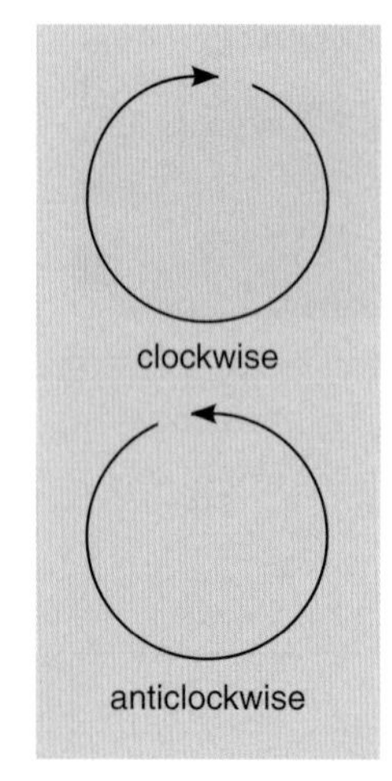

2 ▶ 20 Put each conversation in the correct order. Then listen and check your answers.

1
- [1] Did you say turn the key?
- [ ] Thanks.
- [ ] Yes, that's right.
- [ ] Clockwise.
- [ ] Clockwise or anticlockwise?

2
- [1] What do I do next?
- [ ] Thank you.
- [ ] OK. Which one is the start button?
- [ ] Press the start button.
- [ ] It's the green one, on the left.

3
- [1] How do I start the engine?
- [ ] Switch off? Press the big red button here.
- [ ] Press the green button and turn the key.
- [ ] Thanks.
- [ ] And how do I stop it?

Speaking **3** Work in pairs. Student A look at illustration A on this page. Student B look at illustration B on page 68. Write down what each control is for. Then take turns to explain your illustration. Use these questions to help you.

What's this for?
What does this do?
What's this switch/button/joystick for?
How do I …?

Reading **4** Read this text about mixing concrete. Are sentences 1–5 *true* (T) or *false* (F)?

> Concrete mixers mix and pour concrete. For small quantities of concrete, hand mixers are ideal. The portable mixer has wheels and uses electricity. It has a small drum which rotates. Concrete transport trucks – or in-transit mixers – transport large quantities of concrete to the site. The drum rotates during transport.
> The chute man pours the concrete down the chute, or uses a pump to get the concrete to difficult locations.
> Sometimes a crane lifts a hopper full of concrete to the job site.

1 Concrete mixers mix and pour concrete. (T / F)
2 For small quantities of concrete, transport trucks are ideal. (T / F)
3 Portable mixers use electricity. (T / F)
4 Cranes lift hoppers full of chute men to the job site. (T / F)
5 In-transit mixers rotate during transport. (T / F)

Vocabulary **5** Label photos A–F with the equipment in the box.

chute	concrete pump	concrete transport truck
hand mixer	hopper	portable mixer

____

____

____

____

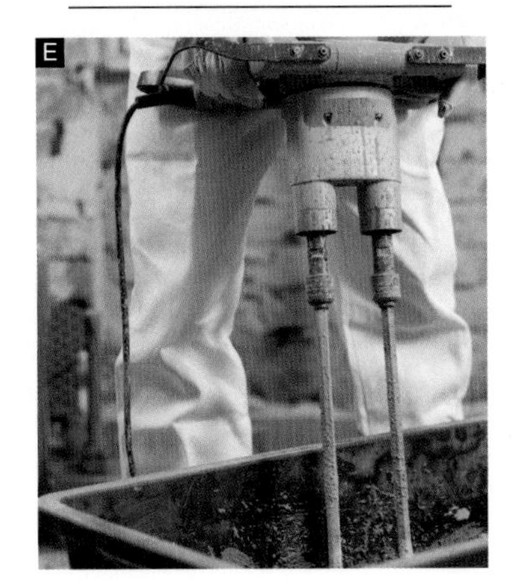

____

____

Speaking **6** Work in pairs. Look at the photos in 5. Make three sentences about each photo. Then compare your sentences with another pair.

On site

Listening **1** 21 Listen and write the conversation number next to each word or phrase. There is one extra word or phrase.

1 boom ______
2 concrete ______
3 sand ______
4 base plates ______
5 hard hat ______
6 flask ______
7 hopper ______
8 remote control ______

2 Put these words in the correct order to make sentences. Then listen again and check your answers.

1 A: Where's the sand?
B: (1) I / the / on / think / it's / way
A: I hope so.

2 A: Where are the base plates?
B: (2) they're / sure / the / in / I'm / truck
A: Ah, OK. That makes sense.

3 A: (3) too / the / boom / is / think / high / I
B: Ah, yes, you're right. Use the radio and speak to the operator.
A: OK. Good idea.

4 A: I think the concrete is too hard.
B: I don't think so. (4) looks / it / to / me / OK
A: Are you sure?
B: OK, go and ask Jim.
A: Will do.

5 A: Where's your hard hat?
B: Over there. Why?
A: Go and get it. (5) this / you / wear / hard / must / area / a / hat / in
B: OK. Here it is.

6 A: We have a problem. (6) hopper / hole / there's / in / a / the
B: John's in the house. He's a welder. Ask him to fix it.
A: Good idea. Thanks.
B: You're welcome.

7 A: (7) don't / flask / the / touch
B: Why? Is it yours?
A: No, it's Norman's.
B: Fair enough.

Speaking **3** Work in pairs. You're on a construction site. Take turns to start a conversation using one of the phrases in the box. Then repeat with a new partner.

How do I ...? I think the ... . What does ...? Where's the ...? Where are the ...?

A: Where's the remote control?
B: I think it's in the truck.
A: OK, thanks.
B: You're welcome.

Review

Writing **1** Write one similarity and one difference between a mobile crane and a tower crane.

1 similarity: ________ 2 difference: ________

2 Put these words in the correct order to make questions.

1 what's / for / this / ?
2 did / you / the / turn / say / key / ?
3 how / I / boom / extend / do / the / ?
4 did / you / move / say / joystick / the / ?
5 what / this / does / do / ?
6 is / this / button / the / start / ?
7 does / this / motor / the / start / ?
8 is / a / key / there / ?

3 Match words 1–6 to definitions a–f.

1 hand mixer
2 portable mixer
3 concrete transport truck
4 chute
5 concrete pump
6 hopper

a) a piece of equipment to get the concrete from the mixer to the job site ______
b) a lightweight machine with a drum for mixing concrete ______
c) a hand tool for mixing concrete ______
d) a vehicle for transporting concrete ______
e) a container for concrete ______
f) a machine to push concrete along a pipe ______

4 Read these instructions for a crane control unit and answer questions 1–4.

The control unit has three levers. The one on the left raises and lowers the boom. Pull it towards you to raise the boom. Push it away to lower the boom. The lever on the right moves the boom from right to left: right is forward and left is backward. The lever in the middle extends or retracts the boom. Pull it towards you to extend and push it away from you to retract. The red button stops the power.

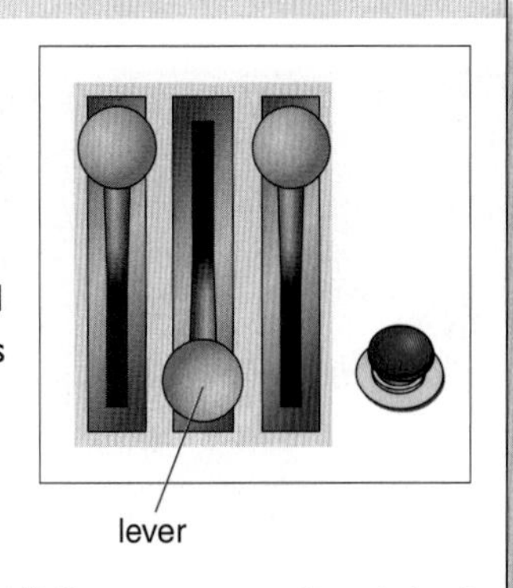

1 How do I make the boom go up?
2 How do I make the boom go to the right?
3 How do I make the boom extend?
4 What does the red button do?

5 Draw a remote control. Put the controls where you like. Then write a description of it.

4 Building supplies

- talk about building materials
- describe problems on site
- order materials
- check stock items
- talk about insulation
- change a customer order/delivery

Building materials

Reading **1** Read these extracts from suppliers' websites and match extracts 1–6 to photos A–F.

1 Thomson's Aggregates: ______

We offer a wide range of construction aggregates, including gravel and sand. We also stock concrete mix.

2 Watson's Goods Ltd: ______

We specialise in acoustic, thermal and fire protection insulation for walls and floors.

3 Morris and Sons Ltd: ______

Our timber comes in a range of standard sizes, but can also be made to order. It is perfect for flooring, roofing and general building work. We also stock plywood and chipboard.

4 Williams Brothers: ______

We design, produce and install high quality steel staircases, gates and railings made to your specifications. We also have a range of standard products.

5 Shockingly Good!: ______

We supply a wide range of electrical products, cables, alarm systems, plugs, sockets, conduits (PVC and steel) and other electrical fittings.

6 Penter's Paint Supplies: ______

We supply everything you need to paint, including brushes, rollers, clothing, spray equipment and, of course, paint.

A

B

C

D

E

F

2 Write three things these suppliers sell.

1 Penter's Paint Supplies
2 Thomson's Aggregates
3 Williams Brothers
4 Watson's Goods Ltd
5 Shockingly Good!
6 Morris and Sons Ltd

Vocabulary **3** Choose the best word to complete these word pairs.

1	acoustic	a) gravel	b) insulation	c) work
2	concrete	a) insulation	b) mix	c) equipment
3	construction	a) sizes	b) railings	c) aggregate
4	electrical	a) aggregate	b) fittings	c) sizes
5	thermal	a) insulation	b) sizes	c) gates
6	alarm	a) systems	b) aggregate	c) mix
7	steel	a) insulation	b) mix	c) staircase

4 Complete these phrases with the words in the box.

everything order standard wide your

1 a range of ________ sizes
2 ________ you need
3 made to ________ specifications
4 a ________ range of products
5 made to ________

5 Label photos A–K with the words in the box.

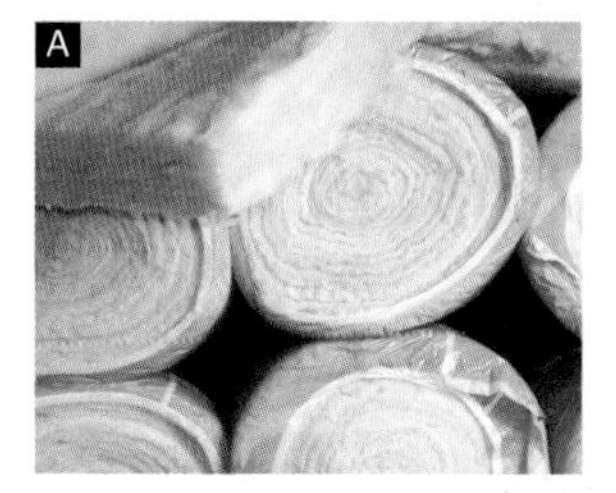

____

____

____

____

____

____

____

____

____

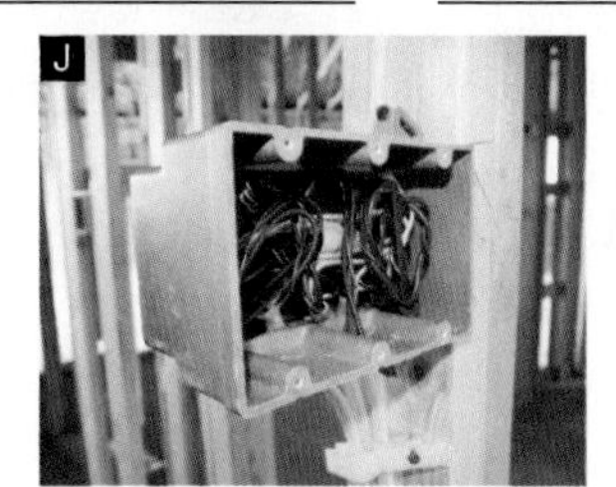

____

____

chipboard electrical fittings fire alarm floor boards gate gravel path insulation railings roofing steel fire escape timber

Speaking **6** Work in small groups. Think about suppliers you know or use. What products do they sell? Discuss.

Materials

Listening **1** ▶ 22 Listen to this telephone conversation and choose the correct answer.

1 Who are Smith and Sons? a) the supplier b) the customer
2 Who are Apex Building? a) the supplier b) the customer

2 Listen again and complete this email.

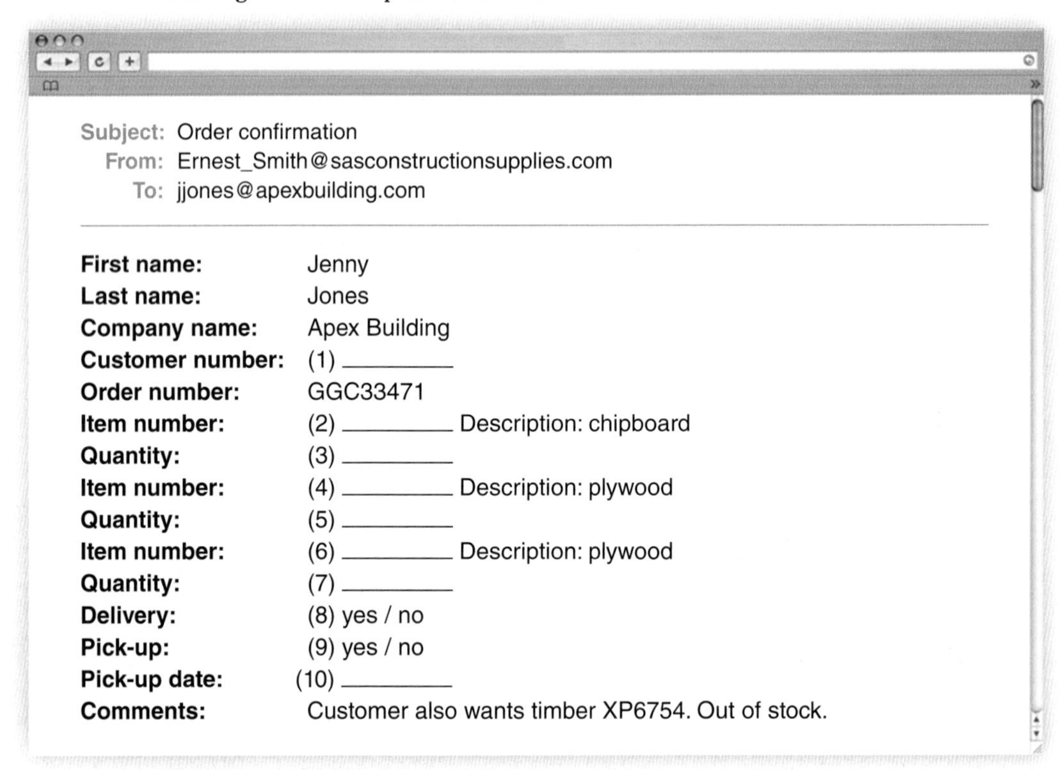

Subject: Order confirmation
From: Ernest_Smith@sasconstructionsupplies.com
To: jjones@apexbuilding.com

First name:	Jenny
Last name:	Jones
Company name:	Apex Building
Customer number:	(1) ________
Order number:	GGC33471
Item number:	(2) ________ Description: chipboard
Quantity:	(3) ________
Item number:	(4) ________ Description: plywood
Quantity:	(5) ________
Item number:	(6) ________ Description: plywood
Quantity:	(7) ________
Delivery:	(8) yes / no
Pick-up:	(9) yes / no
Pick-up date:	(10) ________
Comments:	Customer also wants timber XP6754. Out of stock.

3 ▶ 23 Listen to the follow-up phone call. What is new?

4 Look at audio scripts 22 and 23 on pages 74–75. Underline useful phrases for telephone conversations.

Vocabulary **5** Underline the correct words or phrases in *italics* to complete these conversations.

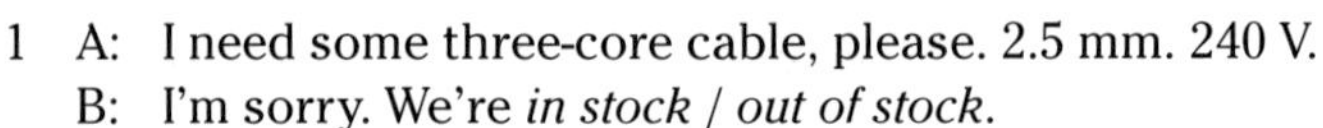

1 A: I need some three-core cable, please. 2.5 mm. 240 V.
B: I'm sorry. We're *in stock / out of stock*.

2 A: I want to order some timber.
B: Yes, of course. What's your *customer number / order number*, please?

3 A: Do you have transport?
B: No, I'm sorry. I don't.
A: No problem. We organise *delivery / pick-up*. Where is the site?

4 A: Hello again.
B: Hello. Can I *place an order / change an order*, please? We need three bags of sand, not thirty.
A: No problem at all.

Speaking **6** Work in pairs. Practise a telephone conversation between a supplier and a buyer. Use the words and phrases in 5 to help you.

A: I'd like to place an order.
B: Certainly. What's your customer number?

A

B

C

Listening

7 ▶ 24 Listen to the conversation and answer these questions.

1 What three things does Isaac want?
2 What two things does Alex give Isaac?

8 Match 1–4 to a–d to complete the conversations.

1 How's it going?
2 Let's see. Here you are.
3 Can I borrow your drill?
4 Do you have an extension cable?

a) No, I'm sorry. It's broken.
b) Good, thanks. And you?
c) Thank you very much.
d) Yes, I think I do.

9 Practise the question form *Do you have …?* Start with question 1. Then change the part of the question in **bold** each time. Write three more questions.

1 Do you have a spare **roll of insulating tape** in your toolbox?
2 Do you have a spare **box of plugs** in your toolbox?
3 Do you have a spare box of plugs in your **truck**?

Language

Making requests

Do you have a spare roll of insulating tape? Yes, I do./No, I don't.	*Does Alex have a three-core cable? Yes, he does./No, he doesn't.*	*Can I borrow your drill? Yes, of course./No, I'm sorry. I'm using it.*

Speaking

10 Work in pairs. Student A look at the information on this page. Student B look at the information on pages 68–69.

Student A

Read this list. Check with Student B that the items are in stock. Then ask to borrow the items you need.

Check stock:

- 12 m extension cable – 3
- 5A/250 V plug – 3
- 20 mm flexible metal conduit – 25 m
- 3G power cable – 30 m
- 18 mm x 30 m PVC insulating tape – 3 rolls

You have:

- spare grey paint
- two brushes
- a roller

You need to borrow:

- spray equipment (for painting)

A: Do you have three 12-metre extension cables?
B: Yes, we do. We have seven in stock.
A: What about conduits?
B: Yes, we have conduits. What type?

A: Can I borrow …?
B: Yes, no problem.

Insulation

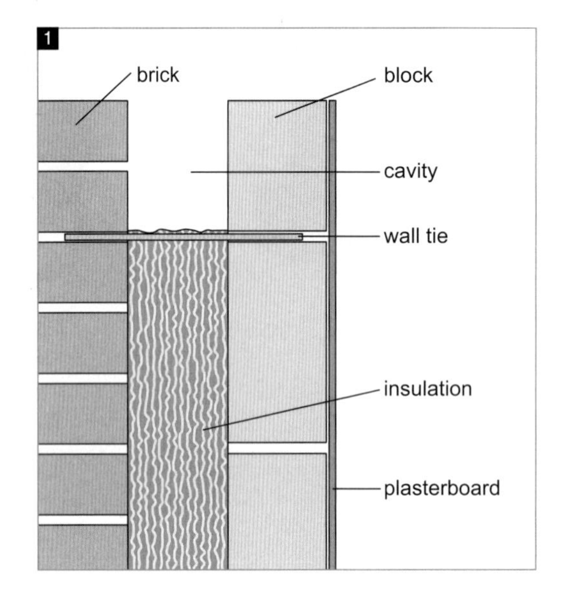

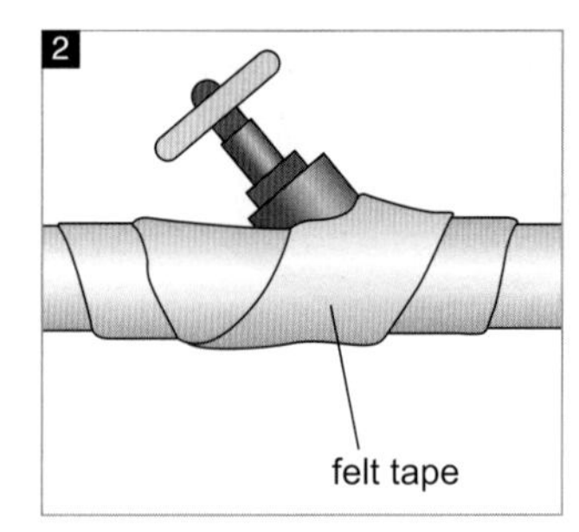

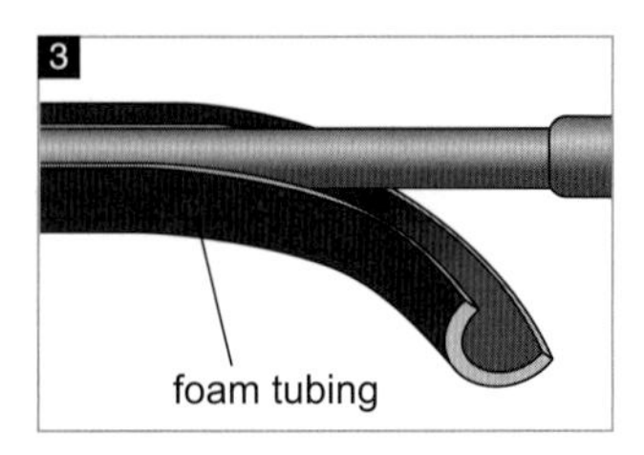

Listening

1 25 Listen to and read the beginning of a conversation between a client and a building contractor and choose the correct answer.

1 Which speaker is the client? (A / B)
2 Which speaker is the building contractor? (A / B)

A: Can you tell me about wall insulation?
B: Sure. There are two types of wall insulation: cavity and solid. Both types provide thermal and acoustic insulation.
A: What's the difference?
B: Let me explain. Sometimes walls are solid, so the insulation is on the outside of the wall. This is solid wall insulation.

2 26 Read the rest of the conversation and put it in the correct order. Then listen and check your answers.

☐ Yes, exactly.
☐ Sometimes walls have two parts: an inner wall and an outer wall. Cavity wall insulation means that the insulation material is inside the wall.
[1] And cavity wall insulation?
☐ Ah, OK. So solid wall is outside and cavity wall is inside?
☐ I see. Thank you.
☐ What about pipes?
☐ OK, I understand. And what types of insulation do you use for cavity wall insulation?
☐ Our company uses three types of cavity wall insulation to fill the gap: foam, mineral wool, or polystyrene beads.
☐ For pipes, we normally use felt tape or foam tubing.

3 Are these statements *true* (T) or *false* (F)? Correct the false statements.

1 Solid wall insulation is used to provide thermal insulation. (T / F)
2 Felt tape is used as cavity wall insulation. (T / F)
3 Cavity wall insulation goes between the inner and outer walls. (T / F)
4 Foam tubing is used to insulate pipes. (T / F)
5 Polystyrene beads are used to insulate pipes. (T / F)

Language

Used to/Used as/Used for

Used to is followed by a verb.	*Solid wall insulation is **used to provide** thermal insulation.*
Used as/used for is followed by a noun or adjective + noun.	*Polystyrene beads are **used as** cavity wall insulation.* *Felt tape is **used for** pipes.*

4 Complete these sentences with *to*, *as* or *for*.

1 Foam tubing is used ________ insulate pipes.
2 Foam tubing is used ________ pipe insulation.
3 Plasterboard is used ________ cover the inner wall.
4 Wall ties are used ________ hold the inner and outer walls together.
5 Polystyrene beads are used ________ cavity wall insulation.

5 Look at the illustrations on page 32. Listen again to recording 26 in 2 and answer these questions.

1 Look at illustration 1. Is it solid wall insulation or cavity wall insulation? ________
2 What three materials are used in cavity wall insulation? ________, ________ or ________
3 What two types of insulation are used for pipes? ________ or ________
4 Which word in the conversation means *cavity*? ________

Speaking **6** Work in pairs and have two telephone conversations. Student A look at the information on this page. Student B look at the information on page 69.

Student A

1 You work for a supplier. Here is an extract of your email to a customer. Phone the customer and tell him/her that Supamat 56 is out of stock. Delivery is next week. Supamat 87 is in stock. You can deliver tomorrow.

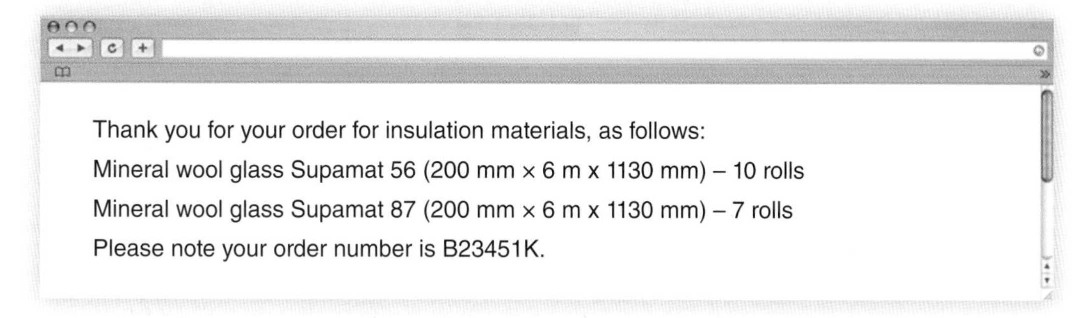
Thank you for your order for insulation materials, as follows:
Mineral wool glass Supamat 56 (200 mm × 6 m x 1130 mm) – 10 rolls
Mineral wool glass Supamat 87 (200 mm × 6 m x 1130 mm) – 7 rolls
Please note your order number is B23451K.

2 There is a problem with the customer's order. Answer his/her call.

Problems on site

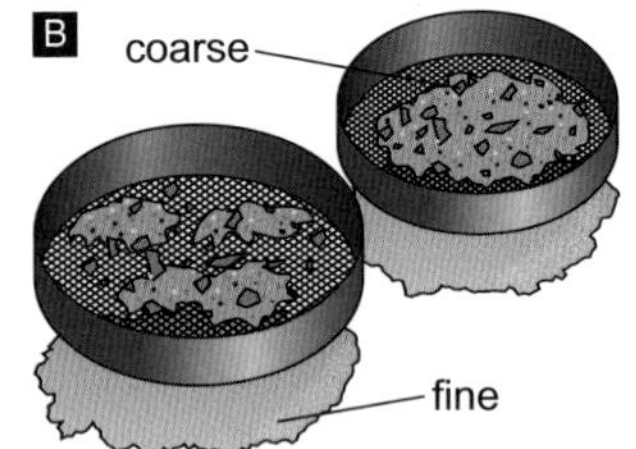

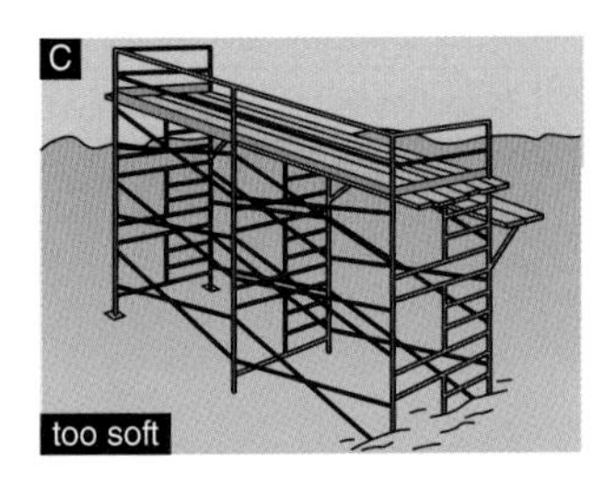

Listening

1 27 Listen to two engineers talking on a building site. What do they say about these things? Choose the correct answer in *italics*.

1 concrete, second floor: *liquid / solid*
2 concrete, first floor: *liquid / solid*
3 paint: *wet / dry*
4 concrete aggregate: *too fine / too coarse*
5 scaffolding: *light / heavy*
6 ground: *too soft / too hard*
7 toolboxes: *too big / too small*

Vocabulary

2 Choose the adjective in *italics* that doesn't go with the noun.

1 *soft / hard / coarse* ground
2 *liquid / heavy / wet* scaffolding
3 *dry / hot / soft* concrete
4 *fine / soft / coarse* aggregate
5 *wet / fine / liquid* paint
6 *big / heavy / soft* toolbox

Language

Too/Not enough

We use **too** + adjective to say that something is more than you want it to be.	*The ground is **too** soft.*
We use **not** + adjective + **enough** to say that you want something to be more than it is.	*The aggregate is **not** fine **enough**.*

3 Complete this conversation with the words in the box.

coarse coffee deliver order soft

A: Problems, problems. I need a(n) (1) ________ .
B: What's up?
A: Thomson's is here with the aggregate. They say the ground is too (2) ________ for the truck. They can't (3) ________ to the job site.
B: I see. What's your plan?
A: We're putting mats down. Everyone is helping.
B: Good.
A: And another thing. I think it's the wrong aggregate. It's not (4) ________ enough. Can you call Thomson's and check the (5) ________?

4 Use the adjectives in 1 and 2 to describe 1–6.

1 steel: ________
2 wood: ________
3 glass: ________
4 gravel: ________
5 sand: ________
6 paint (on a wall): ________

Speaking

5 Work in pairs. Make a list of problems on site. Use *too* and *not enough*. Then discuss solutions.

A: The ground is too soft for the scaffolding.
B: We need timber to make mudsills.

A: The gravel is not coarse enough.
B: We need to order new gravel.

Review

Vocabulary **1** Write three types of the following.

1 insulation: ______ , ______ , ______
2 electrical products: ______ , ______ , ______
3 paint supplies: ______ , ______ , ______

2 Write the opposites.

1 heavy ________
2 small ________
3 wet ________
4 cold ________
5 coarse ________

Writing **3** Complete this email from a supplier to a customer with the words in the box.

insulating item number order quantity services spray telephone

Dear Ms Drescher,

Thank you for your (1) ________ call. This is to confirm your (2) ________, number 367.

(3) ________	**Item**	(4) ________
HB392	plywood	7 pieces
ZU3452M	chipboard	5 pieces
HU786	(5) ________ tape	3 rolls
RE3425	three core cable 2.5 mm	16 m
PL998	(6) ________ equipment	1 set

With best wishes,

Ernest Smith

Customer (7) ________

Smith and Sons Construction Supplies

4 Complete this telephone conversation about the email in 3.

A: Hello. Smith and Sons Construction Supplies. Ernest Smith (1) ________ .
B: Hello. Dorotea Drescher here.
A: Oh, hello, Ms Drescher.
B: It's (2) ________ the email.
A: Yes?
B: There's a mistake. We need 60 metres of three-core cable, (3) ________ 16.
A: One moment, (4) ________ . OK. That's item number RE3425?
B: Yes, that's right.
A: OK, no (5) ________ . 60, not 16.
B: (6) ________ you very much.
A: You're welcome. Goodbye.
B: (7) ________ .

5 You are a supplier. Write three sentences about your company and your products.

5 On site

- say what colleagues do/are doing the moment
- give and follow directions
- talk about the weather
- give reasons using *because of*
- talk about food

On-site subcontractors

Listening **1** ▶ 28 Listen to five people. What do they do? Tick ✓ the correct boxes.

	(1) building inspector	(2) roofer	(3) architect	(4) crane operator	(5) plumber
test electrical systems	✓				
maintain crane					
erect scaffolding					
co-ordinate specifications					
install drainage systems					
check buildings					
install roofing systems					
lift equipment					
design buildings					

2 Match a–g to 1–7 to complete the conversations.

1 I'm looking for Susan. ______
2 So, what do you do? ______
3 Excuse me. I'm looking for the supervisor. ______
4 What about maintenance? Do crane operators maintain their cranes? ______
5 Do you know where Manuel and Carlos are? ______
6 Are you looking for Ken? ______
7 What does Ahmed do? ______

a) They're over there. They're taking a break.
b) He's sitting over there. Look, he's waving.
c) She's in the timber yard with Janet. They're checking stock.
d) He's an electrician.
e) Yes, I am. Is he here?
f) I'm a building inspector. I check systems in new buildings.
g) In general, yes. But mechanics help, too.

Language

Present simple and present continuous

We use the **present simple** to talk about things in general.	***I test*** *electrical and plumbing systems.* (That's my job.) ***He designs*** *buildings.* (That's his job. He's an architect.)
We use the **present continuous** to talk about things that are happening now.	***I'm testing*** *the fire alarms.* ***He's checking*** *the stock.*

3 Tick ✓ the sentences that are true for you. Rewrite the other sentences so they become true for you.

1 ☐ I'm sitting in a classroom.
2 ☐ I'm not listening to the radio.
3 ☐ I work on building sites.
4 ☐ I'm wearing a helmet.
5 ☐ I use computers.
6 ☐ I'm drinking tea.
7 ☐ I'm planning my next holiday.

4 Complete this conversation with the correct form of the verbs in brackets.

A: Hi, Geoff. Good to see you.
B: Same to you, Tony.
A: So, why (1) ________ (you/visit) the site? You normally (2) ________ (stay) in your office.
B: Well, (3) ________ (I/look) for Manuel. I have a report for him.
A: I see. I think (4) ________ (Manuel/have) his lunch at the moment.
B: Ah, OK. Do you know where?
A: (5) ________ (he/train) some new apprentices today. (6) ________ (they/work) with scaffolding in Building 4.
B: OK, thanks.
A: You're welcome.

Speaking

5 Work in pairs. Practise this telephone conversation, then create your own conversations using the prompts.

A: Where are **you**?
B: I'm in the **office**.
A: What are **you** doing?
B: I'm **working** on a **drawing**.

1 on site / testing electrical equipment
2 in the restaurant / meeting a client
3 in the supplier's warehouse / collecting timber

Writing

6 Write down five things you do every week.

I install heating equipment. I write reports ...

Directions

Listening **1** 29 Listen to a driver asking for directions from Sparky's Electrical Supplies and follow the route on the map.

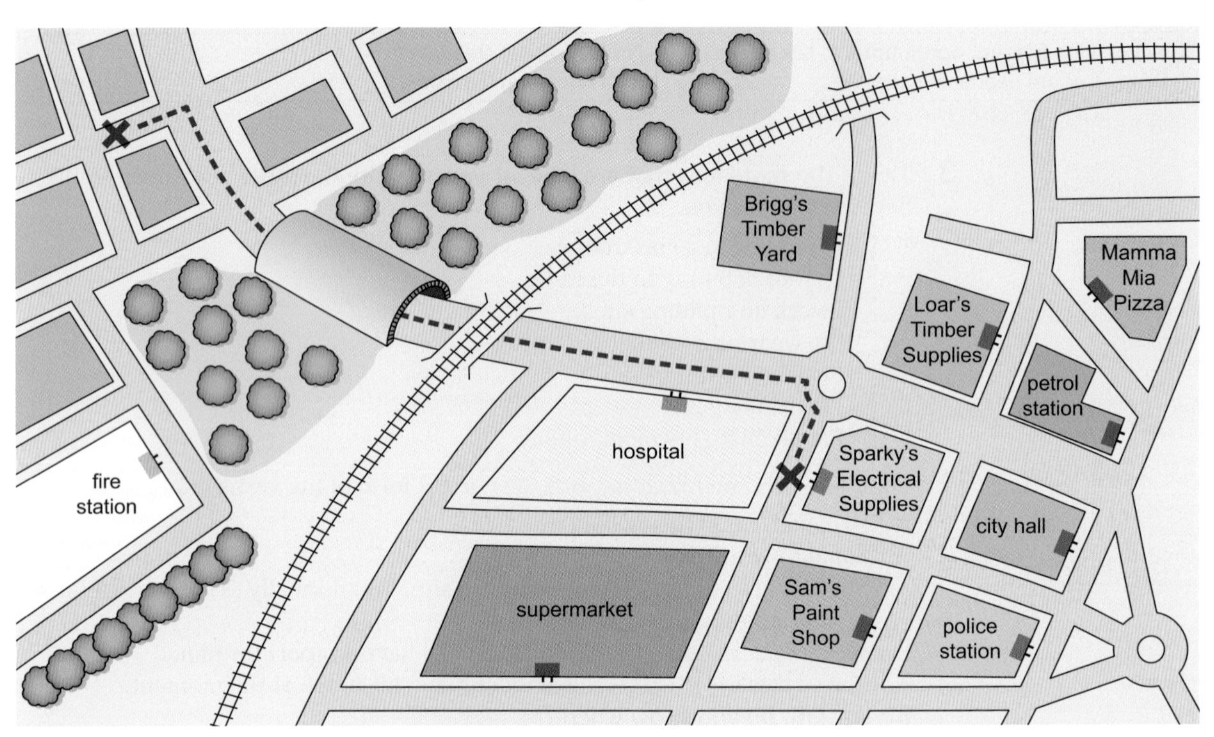

2 Complete these expressions for giving directions with the words in the box. Then listen again and check your answers.

exit miss on past tell

1 Can you ________ me where Mill Street is?
2 Take the first ________ .
3 Then drive ________ the hospital.
4 Mill Street is the second street ________ the left after the tunnel.
5 You can't ________ the entrance to the construction site.

3 Look at the map in 1. Read these directions from Mill Street construction site to Brigg's Timber Yard and put the directions in the correct order.

☐ Go under the railway bridge.
☐ Go through the tunnel.
☐ It's on the left.
☐ Turn right.
☐ *1* Go down Mill Street to the main road.
☐ Turn left at the roundabout.

4 30 Look at the map in 1 again. You're at Brigg's Timber Yard. Listen to the directions. Are they correct or incorrect? Correct the directions as necessary.

Example: *1 incorrect – The hospital is on your left.*

Speaking **5** Work in pairs. Practise giving directions using the map in 1. Start at the city hall.

A: *Can you tell me where the supermarket is?*
B: *Yes. Go past the police station. Turn right. Go past Sam's Paint Shop and it's on your right.*

Listening **6** 31 Listen to this conversation and mark the site manager's office in A.

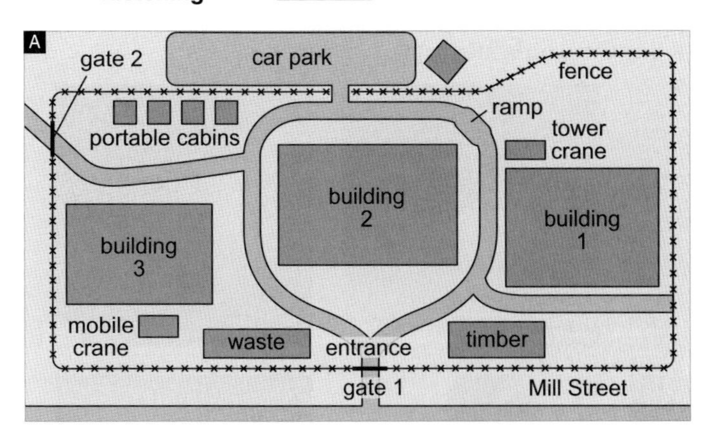

B
portable cabins

Language

Giving directions

Questions:	*Can you help me?/Where's the site manager's office?/How do I get to the conference room?*
Answers:	*Go along the corridor./Take the lift./It's the second door on the right./Go through the fire doors./Go up the stairs./When you come out of the lift, turn right./It's opposite the lift./It's next to the … .*

Speaking **7** Work in pairs. Take turns giving directions. Student A look at the information on this page. Student B look at the information on page 69.

Student A

Look at these floor plans. You are at Reception. Ask Student B how to get to the following.

1 the site management office
2 the first floor conference room
3 the supervisor's office

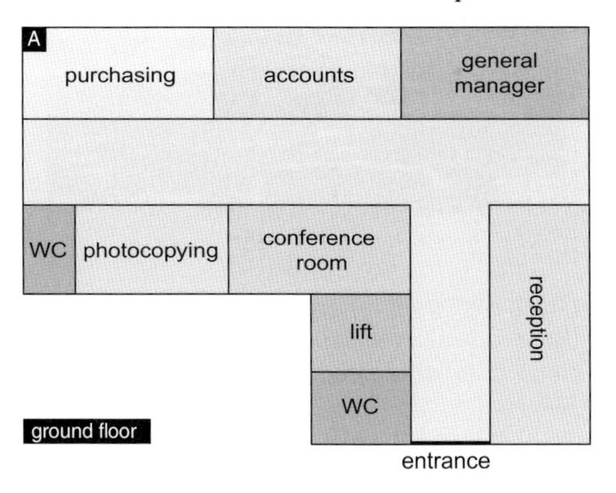

ground floor

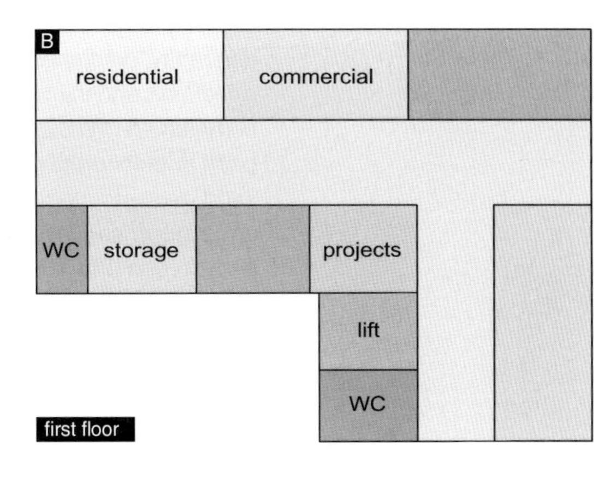

first floor

Weather on site

Vocabulary **1** Look at photos A–F. Say the words aloud.

Listening **2** ▶ 32 Listen and match conversations 1–6 to the weather photos in 1.

Reading **3** Complete this text about extreme weather and construction sites with the words in the box.

cold hot lightning wet wind

Bad weather often causes long delays on construction sites. Building materials behave differently, equipment needs protection and injuries are more common. In (1) ________ weather, paint and concrete dry too fast, sand gets into machines and other equipment, and injuries include dehydration and sunburn. In (2) ________ weather, a big problem is mud. Strong (3) ________ blows things away. (4) ________ can kill. And in (5) ________ weather, workers require special clothing and fingers stick to metal. In extreme weather, accidents are more common. In short, weather is expensive.

4 Read the text in 3 again and match these word pairs from the text.

1 strong	a) clothing
2 big	b) wind
3 special	c) delays
4 wet	d) problem
5 long	e) weather

Reading **5** Put the words in the box in the correct column. Sometimes more than one word is possible.

cloud dehydration lightning mud rain snow sunburn sunny wind

Hot	Cold	Wet

Listening **6** 33 Listen to five telephone conversations and complete this table.

Conversation	Weather	Problem(s)
1	(1) ______	(2) ______
2	(3) ______	(4) ______
3	(5) ______	(6) ______
4	(7) ______	(8) ______
5	(9) ______	(10) ______

Language

Because of

We can use ***because of*** to explain why we can't do something or why something isn't possible.	*How's it going?* *Well, we can't work on the roof at the moment.* *Why not?* ***Because of*** *the rain. It's too dangerous.* *Ah, yes, OK.*

7 Look at audio script 33 on page 76. Underline *because of* in the conversations.

8 Match questions 1–5 to reasons a–e.

1 Why can't you work on the roof? ______
2 Why do you need more sheeting? ______
3 Why can't you work outside? ______
4 Why can't you use the crane? ______
5 Why do you need sunglasses? ______

a) Because of the sand. We need to cover the machines.
b) Because it's too cold. We need better clothing.
c) Because of the sun. It's very bright.
d) Because of the rain. It's too dangerous for the roofers.
e) Because it's too windy. It's difficult to handle the loads.

Speaking **9** Imagine you work on construction sites all over the world. Give examples of problems different types of weather can cause. Discuss these with a partner.

A: *One big problem on building sites is rain.*
B: *Why?*
A: *You can't work on the roof in the rain. It's too dangerous. And the ground is too soft for big trucks.*
B: *And the paint can't dry.*
A: *Yes, good point.*

Food

Vocabulary **1** Read conversations 1–6 and match them to photos A–F. Then complete the conversations with the words in the box.

A

B

C

D

E

F

biscuits	coffee	milk	noodles	sandwiches	soup

1 A: What have you got?
B: Chocolate (1) ________ . Want one? You look hungry.
A: Yes, please. And you're right. I am hungry.
B: There you go.
A: Thanks.

2 A: What are you drinking?
B: Orange juice. Would you like some?
A: No, thanks. I always drink (2) ________ when I'm thirsty.

3 A: There's a takeaway down the road.
B: What do they do?
A: (3) ________ . Different kinds, like cheese and tuna. And they also do other snacks.
B: That sounds like just what I need.

4 A: Would you like some (4) ________?
B: Yes, please.
A: How do you take it?
B: White with sugar, thanks.

5 A: What are you eating?
B: Chicken (5) ________ .
A: Ah. I have fish with rice.

6 A: It's cold today.
B: Yes. Below zero, I think.
A: What's in the flask?
B: (6) ________ .
A: Smells great. Is it chicken?
B: Yes.

Speaking **2** Work in pairs and practise the conversations in 1. What do you usually have for lunch? What are you having today? Discuss with your partner.

3 Work in small groups. You're on a building site. It's lunchtime. Ask your colleagues what they're having for lunch.

Review

Writing **1** Complete this conversation with the correct form of the verbs in brackets.

A: Hi!
B: Can I help you?
A: Yes, I (1) ________ (look for) Saskia Polinski. She's an electrician.
B: Yes, I know Saskia. Today she (2) ________ (work) in that building over there. She (3) ________ (install) a lighting system on the ground floor.
A: Thanks.
B: Just a moment. Isn't that her over there? In the blue jacket? She (4) ________ (carry) a box or something.
A: No, I can't see her.
B: She (5) ________ (walk) past the blue portable cabin.
A: Yes, I think you're right. Thanks.
B: Don't mention it.

2 Answer these questions about the conversation in 1.

1 What does Saskia do?
2 What is Saskia doing? (four things)

3 Look at the map on page 38. Write directions:

1 from the Mill Street construction site to the supermarket.
2 from Sparky's Electrical Supplies to the petrol station.
3 from Brigg's Timber Yard to Mill Street.

4 Write the type of weather that causes the following.

1 dehydration
2 sand to get in machines
3 sheeting to blow away
4 fingers to stick to metal
5 soft ground

5 Write questions for answers 1–4.

1 Because of the snow.
2 Because it's too wet.
3 Because of the wind.
4 Because it's too hot.

6 Complete this email with what you had for lunch.

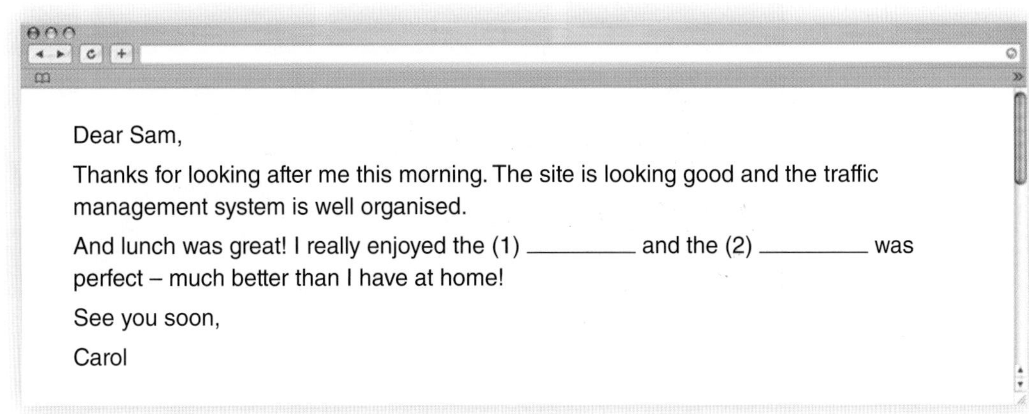

Dear Sam,

Thanks for looking after me this morning. The site is looking good and the traffic management system is well organised.

And lunch was great! I really enjoyed the (1) ________ and the (2) ________ was perfect – much better than I have at home!

See you soon,

Carol

7 Work in small groups. Brainstorm lists of things to eat and drink.

6 Health and safety

- **identify warning signs**
- **complete a vehicle safety checklis**
- **explain injuries**
- **talk about waste disposal colour codes**

Warning signs

Vocabulary **1** Look at these signs. What do they mean? Complete the sentences for signs 1–6 with the words in the box.

1 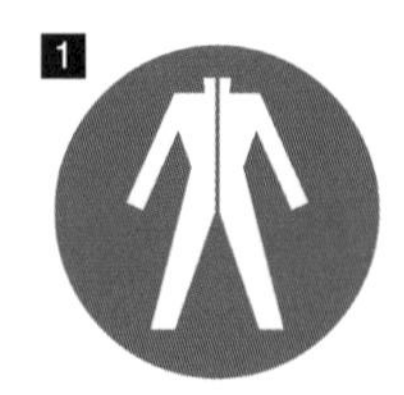
2 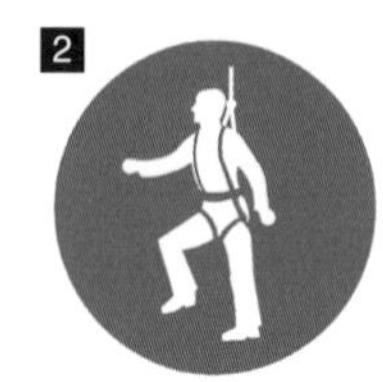
3 
4 
5 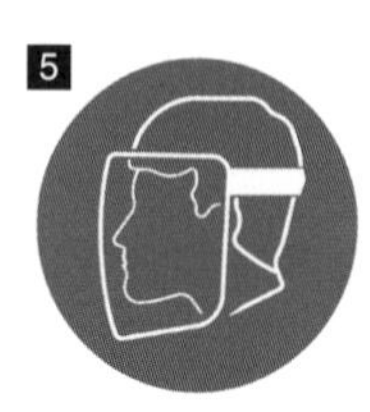
6 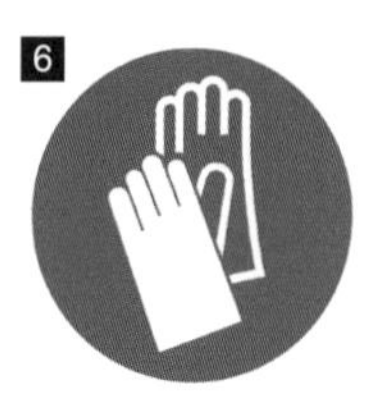

a harness	a mask	ear protection	gloves
protective clothing	safety glasses		

1 You must wear ________ .
2 You must wear ________ .
3 You must wear ________ .
4 You must wear ________ .
5 You must wear ________ .
6 You must wear ________ .

2 Here are some other signs. What is the difference between these signs and the signs in 1?

A 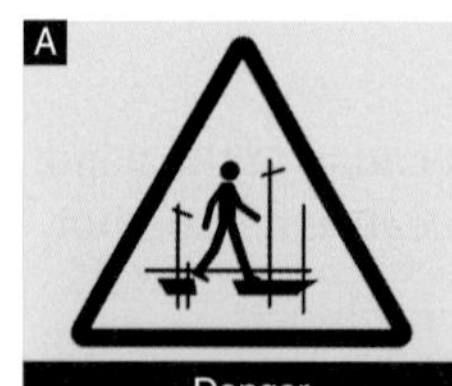

B 

C 

D 

E 

F 

G 

H 

3 Read these sentences. What sign is needed? Look at the signs in 2 and write the sign letter for 1–8.

1 There are men working on the roof today. ______
2 The new security company uses dogs. ______
3 There are power cables near the fence. ______
4 There's a lot of debris on the ground. ______
5 We're erecting the scaffolding this afternoon. ______
6 We're using the crane today. ______
7 We're moving the timber today. ______
8 There's oil on the ground. ______

4 Use clues 1–9 to fill in the squares. What health and safety advice do you read in the column?

Clues:

1 overhead ________
2 ________ surface
3 falling ________
4 suspended ________
5 ________ hazard
6 stand ________
7 ________ lift truck
8 ________ dog
9 safety ________

Listening **5** 34 Listen to eight conversations and match them to the signs in 2.

1 Conversation 1	a) A
2 Conversation 2	b) B
3 Conversation 3	c) C
4 Conversation 4	d) D
5 Conversation 5	e) E
6 Conversation 6	f) F
7 Conversation 7	g) G
8 Conversation 8	h) H

6 Look at these photos. What are A–E called? Listen again and check your answers.

A

____

B

____

C
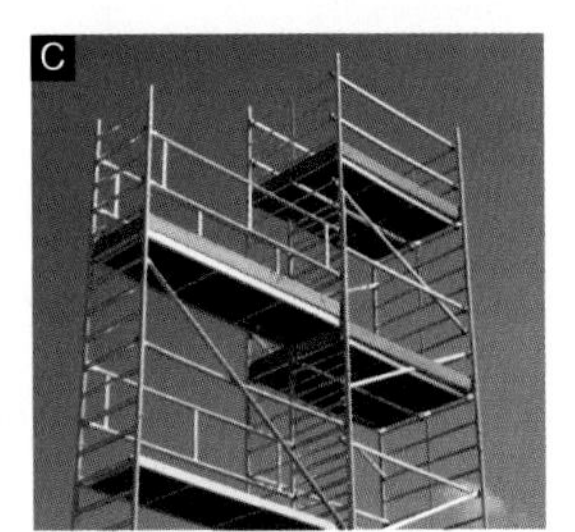
____

D
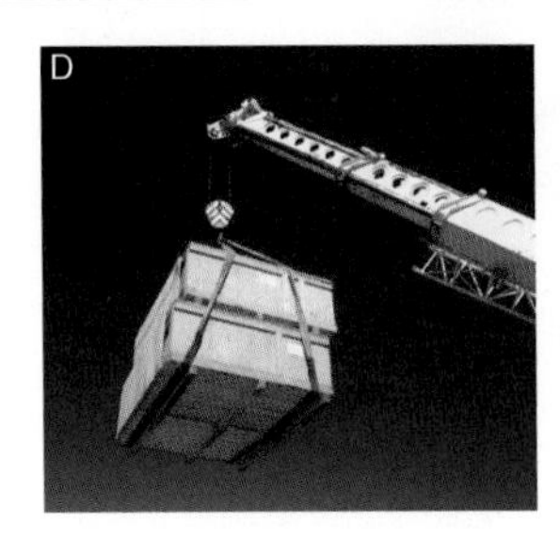
____

E

____

Speaking **7** Work in pairs. What other safety signs do you know/see on site? Discuss with your partner. Take turns to say what the signs mean.

Site safety

Vocabulary **1** Look at this illustration. Circle the health and safety problems you see.

2 You are an inspector. Look at the illustration in 1 again. Tick (✓) good or cross (✗) bad for 1–6 in this report. Then write the problem for each using the words in the box.

boots children fall helmet ladder mask oil skip trip welding

RB Johnson Construction		Good	Bad	Problem(s)
1	Waste			
2	PPE			
3	Access			
4	Vehicles			
5	Signs			
6	Equipment			

Speaking **3** Work in pairs. Compare your reports in 2.

4 Find a new partner. Take turns to describe a problem on a construction site. Is the problem in the illustration in 1?

Vocabulary **5** Look at this illustration. Say the words aloud. Then close your book, draw an illustration of a fork lift truck and label it.

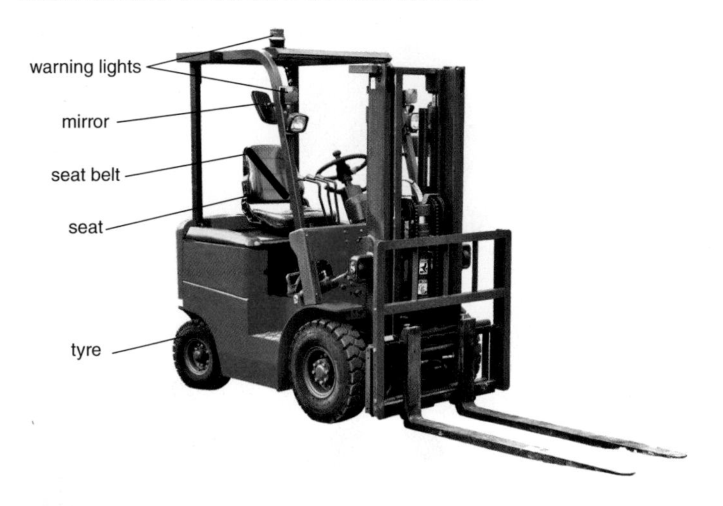

Listening **6** 35 Listen to this conversation. Write the vehicle number then complete the checklist with a tick (✓) or cross (✗).

Fork lift Daily Inspection Checklist

Vehicle number: ______

✓ = OK ✗ = action needed	Lights	Mirrors	Seat	Seat belt	Tyres	Fluids	Battery	Documents
Tuesday								

7 Listen again and describe the three problems with the vehicle.

Speaking **8** Work in pairs. Student A look at the information on this page. Student B look at the information on page 70.

Student A

Read the list of faults for vehicle GH675 and explain them to Student B. Then make notes about the faults for vehicle JK893.

✓ = OK ✗ = action needed	Lights	Mirrors	Seat	Seat belt	Tyres	Fluids	Battery	Documents
GH675	✓	✗	✓	✓	✗	✓	✗	✗
JK893								

First aid

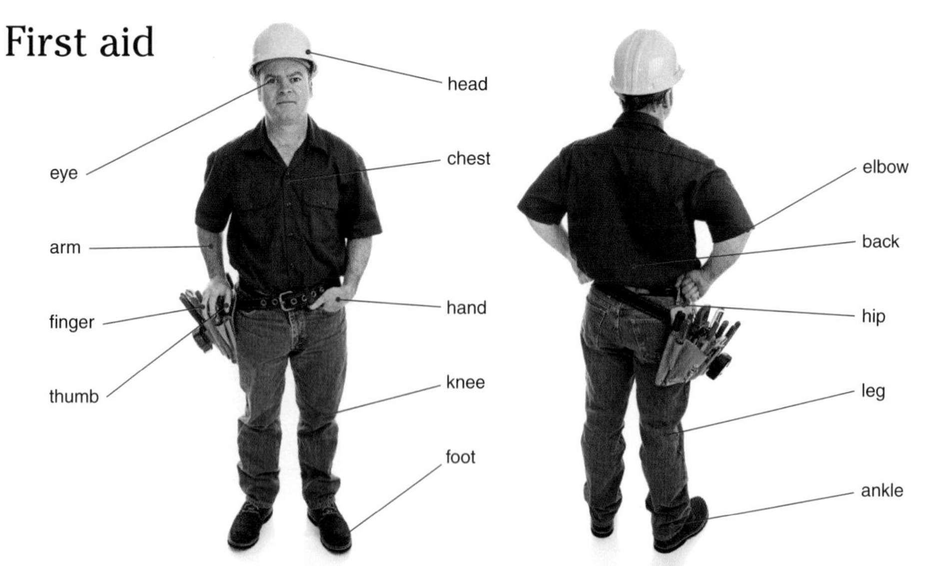

Vocabulary

1 ▶ 36 Listen to six conversations about injuries on site and match 1–6 to a–f to complete the sentences.

1 He sprained	a) his arm.
2 He broke	b) his back.
3 He burnt	c) her finger.
4 He hurt	d) his hand.
5 She cut	e) his ankle.
6 The pallet crushed	f) his knee.

Language

Past simple: *be*

We use the past simple of **be** to talk about the past.	*I/He/She/It **was**/**wasn't** in the site manager's office yesterday.* *We/You/They **were**/**weren't** here this morning.*

Past simple

We use the **past simple** to talk about actions and situations that started and finished in the past.

To form the past simple of **regular verbs**, we add ***-ed*** to the verb.	*I sprain**ed** my ankle.* *The pallet crush**ed** his hand.*
Some verbs do not form the past simple with *-ed*. They are **irregular** (e.g. *go* → *went, buy* → *bought, meet* → *met*, etc.).	*He **fell** off the scaffolding. (fall → fell)* *He **broke** his arm. (break → broke)*

2 Read this extract from an accident report and underline the verbs in the past simple. Which verbs are regular?

ACCIDENT REPORT

RB Johnson Construction

Name: Michel Kempinski **Date:** 7th November **Location:** Mill Street

Description of incident: I was in the site manager's office yesterday. There was a problem with some waste management paperwork. The site manager told me to check the skips in the yard. I counted the skips and found there were only six, not eight. Then I saw the accident. Harry tried to lift a skip with his crane. The load was too heavy and the crane tipped over. It crashed into the scaffolding that we erected yesterday. Four men were hurt. We called the emergency services. They sent two ambulances.

Vocabulary **3** Tick ✓ the items you need to treat a cut finger.

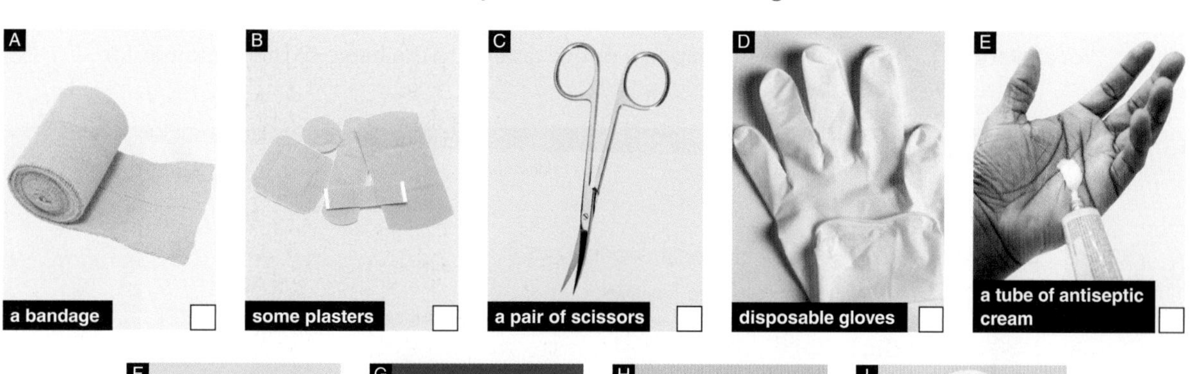

4 Put these sentences for the treatment of a cut finger in the correct order.

- [ ] Clean the cut under running water.
- [ ] Cover the cut with a dressing or plaster.
- [ ] Put on disposable gloves.
- [1] Wash your hands.
- [ ] Dry the cut using a dressing or cotton wool.

5 Imagine a worker cut his finger yesterday. Write down how you treated it. Use the verbs in the box to help you.

cleaned	covered	dried	put on	washed

Listening **6** 37 Listen and compare. Is anything different to the way you treated the finger in 5?

7 38 Listen to a health and safety officer ordering supplies from a medical supplier for the first aid kit and complete this list.

* two rolls of (1) ________
* one tube of antiseptic (2) ________
* three boxes of (3) ________
* a couple of packets of (4) ________
* a bottle of (5) ________

Speaking **8** Work in pairs and take turns. Choose one of the injuries in 1. Tell your partner about the injury and explain how it happened. Your partner explains what to do using the phrases in the box.

call an ambulance   get the first aid kit   go to hospital   see the doctor
take an X-ray

A: I cut my finger on some broken glass.
B: OK. I need to get the first aid kit. First, I need to clean the cut ... .

Waste disposal

Vocabulary **1** Read this waste disposal notice and write the name of the container for items 1–7.

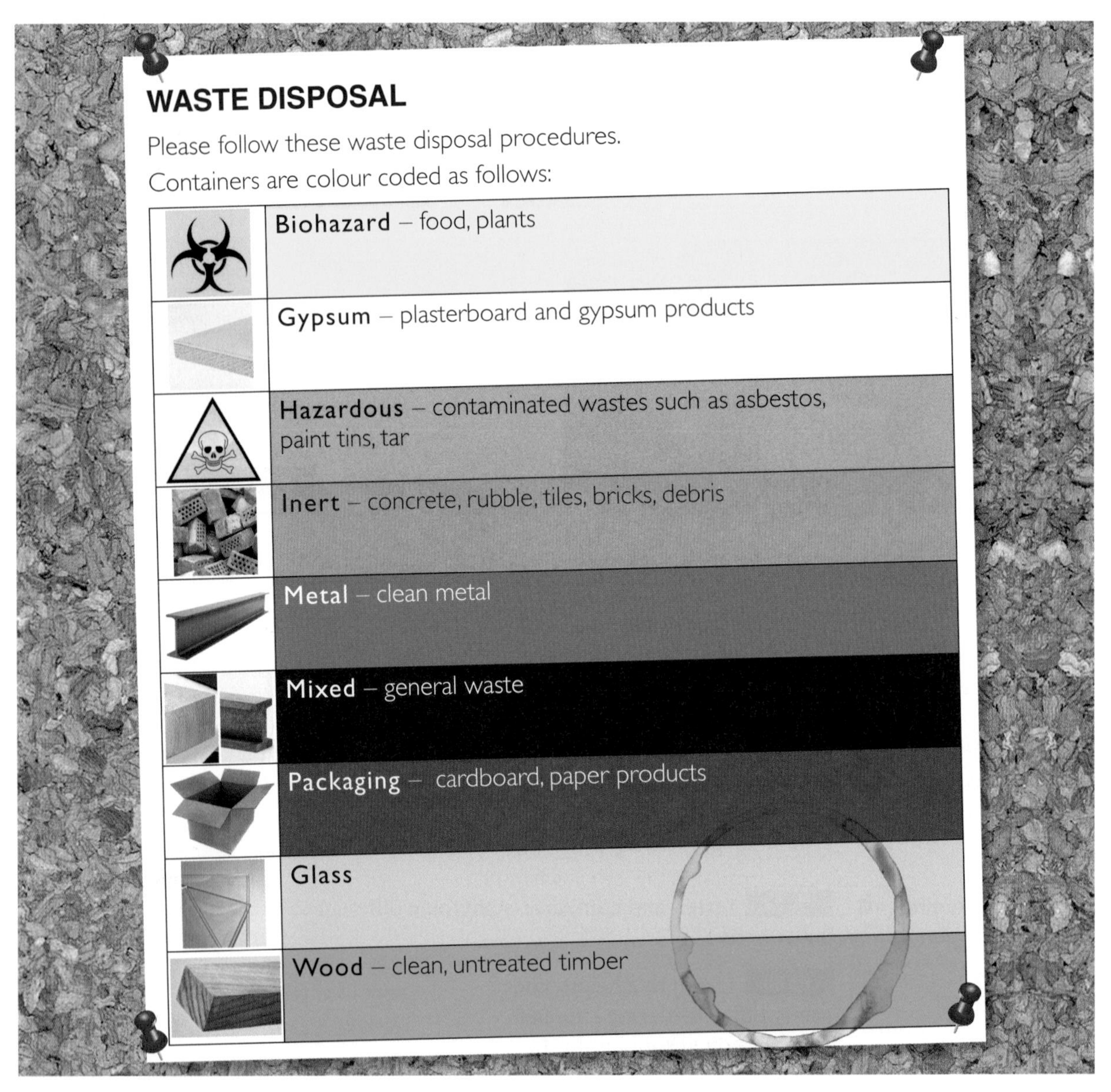

WASTE DISPOSAL
Please follow these waste disposal procedures.
Containers are colour coded as follows:
Biohazard – food, plants
Gypsum – plasterboard and gypsum products
Hazardous – contaminated wastes such as asbestos, paint tins, tar
Inert – concrete, rubble, tiles, bricks, debris
Metal – clean metal
Mixed – general waste
Packaging – cardboard, paper products
Glass
Wood – clean, untreated timber

1 manuals: ________
2 left-over food: ________
3 broken steel pipe: ________
4 paint tins: ________
5 old sheeting: ________
6 tarmac: ________
7 painted wood: ________

2 39 Listen and check your answers to 1.

Speaking **3** Work in small groups. Talk about waste disposal in your area.

A: *We have three skips. One is for debris, one is for paint and one is for general waste.*
B: *What about glass?*
A: *Glass goes in general waste.*

Review

Writing **1** Write the meanings of these signs.

2 Describe the faults on a vehicle you inspected. Use the words in the box.

broken cracked dirty flat leaking missing

3 Write the items you need to treat a cut finger. Then write how to treat it.

4 Read this email about accidents on the Mill Street site and correct the words in **bold**.

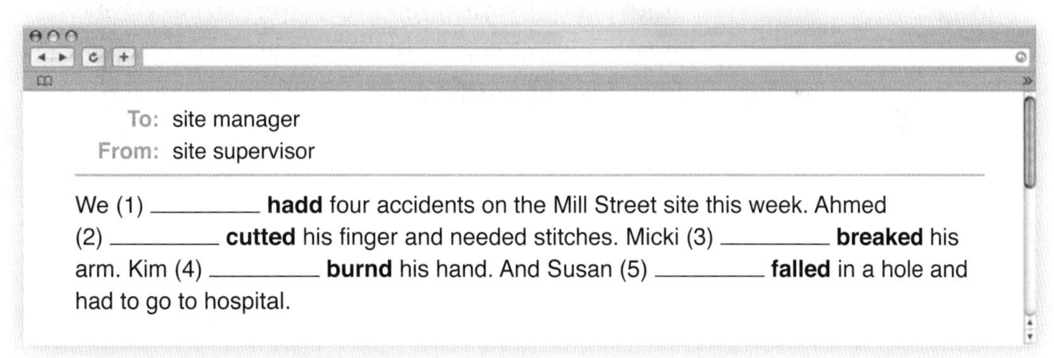

To: site manager
From: site supervisor

We (1) ________ **hadd** four accidents on the Mill Street site this week. Ahmed (2) ________ **cutted** his finger and needed stitches. Micki (3) ________ **breaked** his arm. Kim (4) ________ **burnd** his hand. And Susan (5) ________ **falled** in a hole and had to go to hospital.

5 Use the chart on page 50 to complete this email about waste disposal on a construction site.

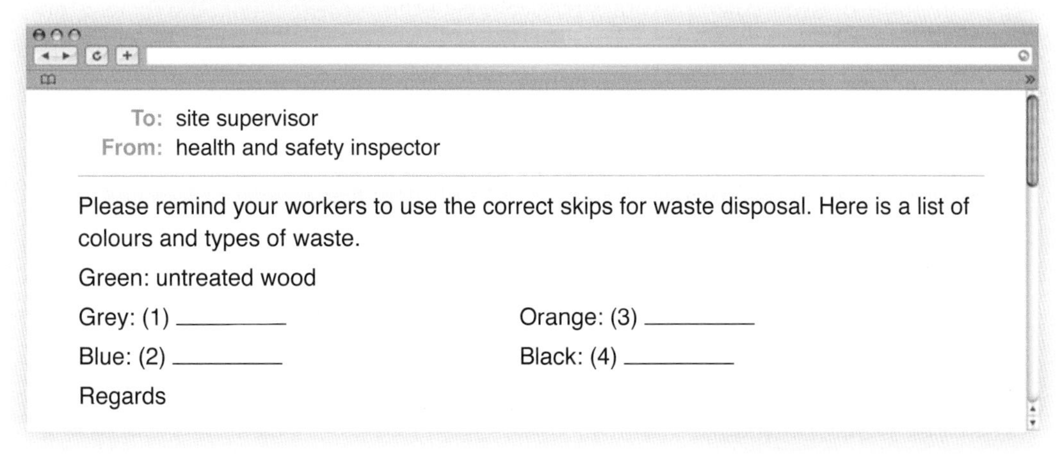

To: site supervisor
From: health and safety inspector

Please remind your workers to use the correct skips for waste disposal. Here is a list of colours and types of waste.

Green: untreated wood

Grey: (1) ________

Blue: (2) ________

Orange: (3) ________

Black: (4) ________

Regards

7 The contractor's office

- welcome clients and explain what staff members do
- discuss projects
- describe structures using dimensi
- describe the shape of constructio
- calculate an area

Clients

Reading **1** Read this email. What is it about?

From: SRamirez@ramco.com
To: Arnold_ Schmidt@gov.co.uk

Dear Mr Schmidt,

Thank you for your email and congratulations on your new job! I confirm I am available on Tuesday for a meeting and look forward to your visit to our offices next Tuesday at 9 a.m. to meet our staff and to discuss the Cambridge Road Hospital project.

With best wishes,

Susana Ramirez

General Manager

RamCo

Listening **2** 40 Listen to five conversations between Arnold Schmidt and Susana Ramirez and answer these questions.

1 Where does Arnold Schmidt work?
2 What is Susana Ramirez in charge of?
3 How does Arnold Schmidt take his coffee?
4 What plan does Susana Ramirez suggest?
5 What time does Arnold Schmidt have to leave?

3 Match 1–5 to a–e to complete the conversations. Listen again and check your answers.

1 Hello. My name's Arnold Schmidt. I'm here to see Susana Ramirez. ______
2 Hello. I'm Susana Ramirez. You must be Mr Schmidt. ______
3 Before we start, would you like coffee? ______
4 How about if I introduce you to the team first? Then we can look at the designs and you can ask any questions you have. ______
5 How long have we got? ______

a) Yes, that's right. Pleased to meet you.
b) Ah, yes. One moment, please. She's expecting you.
c) I have to leave at 11.30. So we've got about an hour.
d) Yes, please. With milk and one sugar, please.
e) That sounds perfect.

4 ▶ 41 Listen to Susana Ramirez introducing her staff. How many employees are there?

5 Listen again and complete this staff directory. Use the words in the box. Who is out of the office?

Bookkeeper	Civil Engineering student	Structural Engineer	Team Assistant

RamCo

RamCo staff directory

Susana Ramirez	General Manager
Kenneth McGarry	Architect
Rowena Murphy	(1) ________
Janet L Jones	Structural Engineer
Timothy Wiseman	Project Manager
Luisa Serrano	Project Manager
Thomas McNamara	(2) ________
Julita Zielinski	(3) ________
Nasim Orgun	(4) ________

Vocabulary

6 Match 1–5 to a–e to make new words or word pairs.

1 team	a) manager
2 engineering	b) keeper
3 project	c) assistant
4 structural	d) student
5 book	e) engineer

7 Put these words in the correct order to make sentences.

1 Rowena / the / all / does / calculations
2 Julita / of / charge / is / in / staff / the / schedule
3 Thomas / next / graduate / hopes / to / year
4 Nasim / the / looks / after / finances
5 the / others / the / all / out / are / at / moment

Speaking

8 Work in small groups and complete the following.

1 Imagine you work together in a general contractor's office. Who does what? Write a staff directory using job titles.
2 Send one person – 'the visitor' – to another 'office' to be introduced to their staff.
3 Introduce the visitor to your staff. Explain the jobs and responsibilities of your staff.

A: *This is … . He/She's responsible for … . At the moment he/she's working on … .*
B: *Pleased to meet you.*
A: *And this is … .*

Projects

Listening **1** 42 Listen to Susana Ramirez and Arnold Schmidt talking about Block A of the Cambridge Road Hospital project and find the things they talk about in A–D.

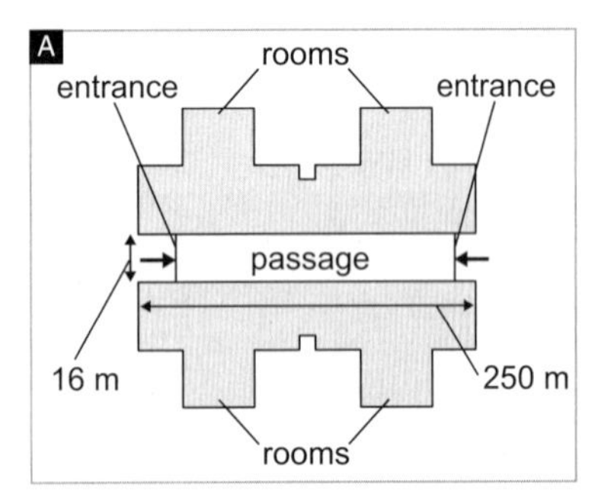

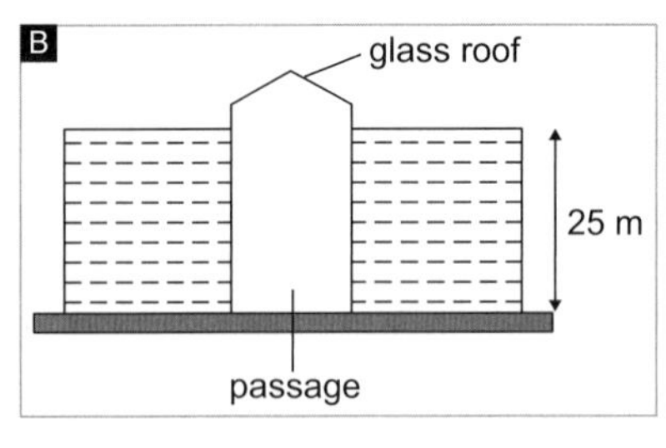

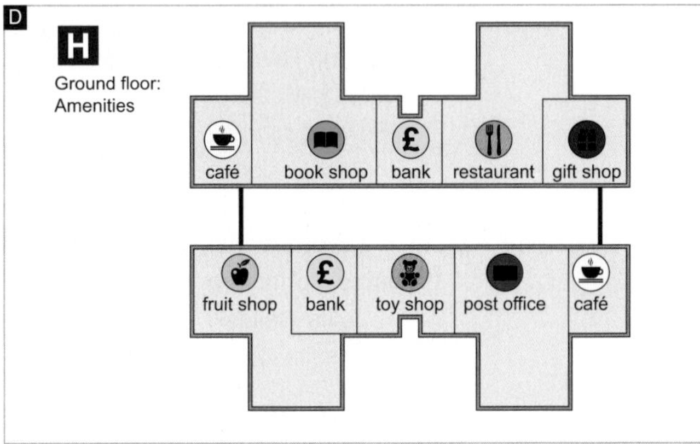

Language

Metric and imperial measurements

The construction industry uses both **metric** (e.g. *cm/m/km*) and **imperial** (e.g. *inches/feet/yards*) measurements.	1 inch = 1" = 2.54 cm 12 inches = 1 foot = 1' 3 feet = 3' = 1 yard 1 m = 3.281'	
You can ask and answer questions about dimensions in different ways:	*How high is it? It's 25 metres high.* OR *What's the height? The height is 25 metres.*	*How wide is it? It's 16 metres wide.* OR *What's the width? The width is 16 metres.*
	How long is it? It's 150 metres long. OR *What's the length? The length is 250 metres.*	*What's the area? It's 25 m^2.* (square metres) *What's the volume? It's 46 m^3.* (cubic metres)

2 Fill in the gaps in the conversation.

A: So tell me about the new project. I hear it has a(n) (1) ________ passage?
B: Yes, that's right. And a(n) (2) ________ roof.
A: How (3) ________ is it?
B: The passage? 16 (4) ________ .
A: How much is that in feet?
B: Oh, about (5) ________ feet.
A: And how long is it?
B: 250 m. Sorry. About (6) ________ yards.
A: Quite a lot of floor space then?
B: Yes. The (7) ________ is 4000 m^2. And don't ask me what that is in feet!

Listening **3** ▶ 43 Listen to three more conversations about Block A of the Cambridge Road Hospital project and complete this table. Then compare your answers with a partner.

Conversation	Topic	Details
1	(1) ________	(2) ________
2	(3) ________	(4) ________
3	(5) ________	(6) ________

Reading **4** Read this newspaper article about the Cambridge Road Hospital project and correct the seven mistakes.

Work on the Cambridge Road Hospital project is going to plan, says Arnold Smith, the government official responsible for the project. The new skyscraper has six floors and is 150 metres long. The design has a central passage with rooms on each side. The passage has different amenities, including shops and restaurants, and a wooden roof. The project manager in charge, Julita Zielinski of RamCo, says that the project includes a new underground car park. A local company, Hingewell Doors, are supplying the doors.

Speaking **5** Work in pairs. Student A look at the information on this page. Student B look at the information on page 70. Exchange information about two buildings.

Student A

Look at this photo and read the information about Taipei 101. Tell Student B about the building. Then listen and take notes about Student B's building.

Taipei 101

This skyscraper is 508 metres high and has 101 floors. An interesting feature is the steel pendulum which hangs from the 92nd floor and acts as a damper against strong winds. It consists of 41 circular steel plates. Each plate is 125 millimetres high. Together they form a 5.5 metre diameter sphere. Every year, there is a race up the 2,046 steps from floors 1 to 91. The record is just under 10 minutes and 30 seconds.

The Burj Khalifa

Height: (1) ________

Dimensions: (2) ________

Number of windows: (3) ________

Rebar: (4) ________

Shapes

Vocabulary

1 44 Listen and write the conversation letter next to the shape. Listen again and complete the table using the words in the box.

I-shaped rectangular sphere square triangular

1 ______	(triangle)	a triangle	a(n) 2 ______ truss
3 ______	(I-shape)	an I-shape	a(n) 4 ______ girder
5 ______	(circle)	a circle	a circular rod
6 ______	(square)	a square	a(n) 7 ______ beam
8 ______	(cylinder)	a cylinder	a cylindrical can
9 ______	(sphere)	a(n) 10 ______	a spherical damper
11 *A*	(rectangle)	a rectangle	a(n) 12 ______ room

2 45 Underline the stress in these words. Then listen and check your answers.

1	cylinder	cylindrical
2	rectangle	rectangular
3	triangle	triangular
4	circle	circular

3 Complete these sentences with words to describe shapes.

1 The pendulum in Taipei 101 is ______ .
2 This page is ______ .
3 My cup of coffee is ______ .
4 A 90° cross-section of a pipe is ______ .
5 Many steel beams are ______ .

Speaking

4 Work in a small group. Make lists of things that are the following shapes.

1 circular
2 rectangular
3 cylindrical
4 square
5 spherical
6 I-shaped
7 triangular

5 Compare your lists in 4 with other groups.

Listening **6** 46 Listen to a structural engineer describing the dimensions of two beams: an I-shaped cross-section and a standard channel cross-section, and a rod. Complete these tables.

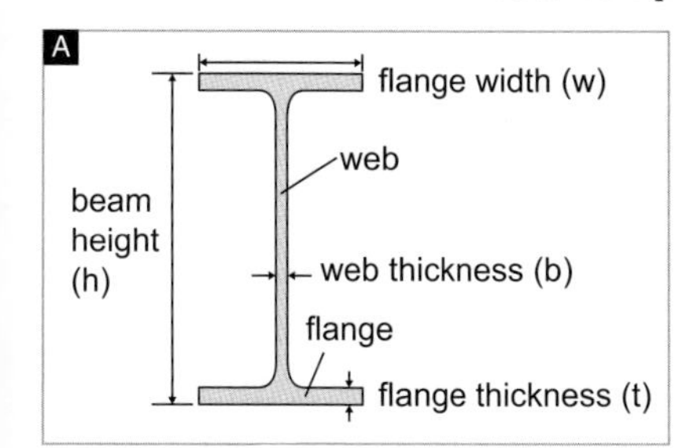

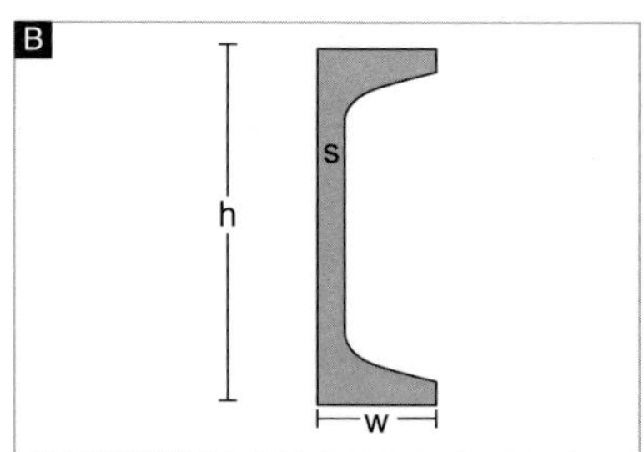

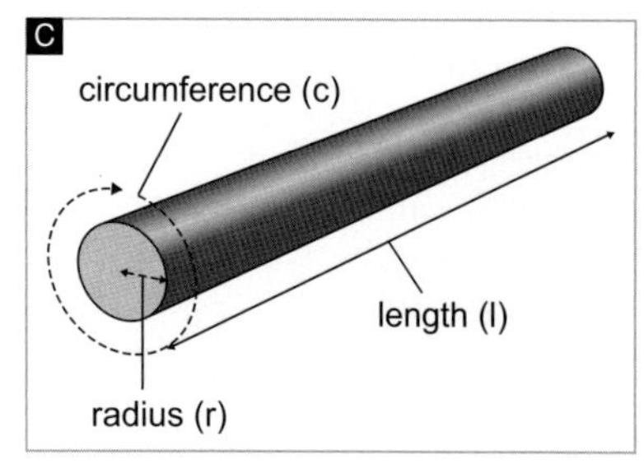

I-shaped cross-section	
Flange width:	(1) ________
Flange thickness:	(2) ________
Web thickness:	(3) ________
Beam height:	(4) ________
Area:	(5) ________

Standard channel cross-section	
Depth (h):	(6) ________
Width (w):	(7) ________
Web thickness (s):	(8) ________
Area:	(9) ________

Rod	
Radius (r):	(10) ________
Length (l):	(11) ________

Language

Expressions

Note how we say dimensions:	3.520 = *three point five two oh* 0.370 = *(nought/zero/oh) point three seven oh* (We do NOT say *three point fifty-two*, or *three point five hundred and twenty*.)
1 inch = approximately 25 millimetres	*This board is 30 × 600. = This board is 30 by 600.*

7 Write these dimensions in words.

1 2.345 2 0.146 3 35.290 4 63.38 5 3.402

Speaking **8** Work in pairs to complete these dimensions. Student A look at the information on this page. Student B look at the information on page 70.

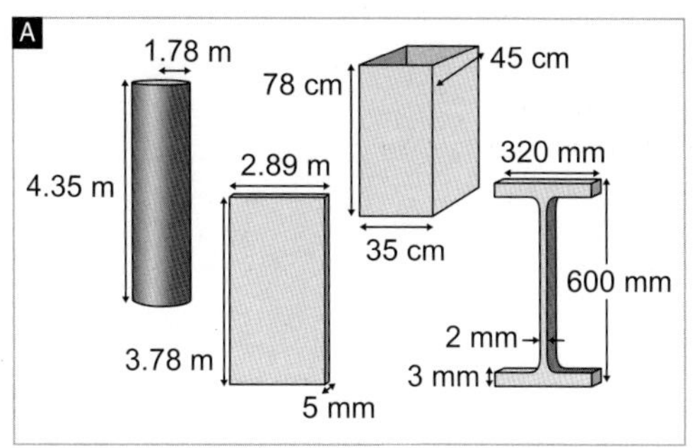

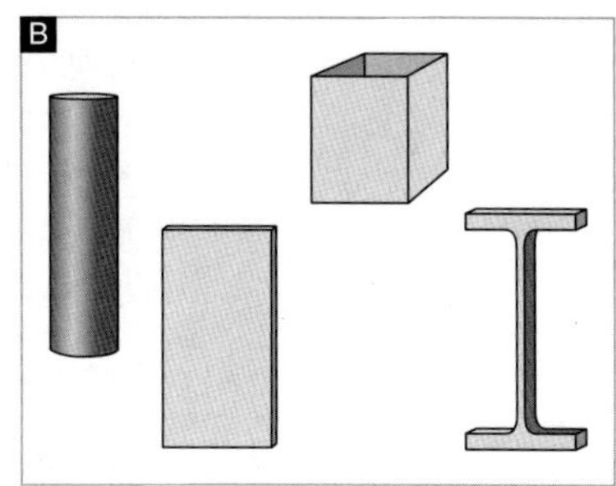

A: What are the dimensions of the rod?
B: It's 4.35 metres long, … .
A: What about the radius?
B: The radius is … .

Calculations

Vocabulary

- area of a circle = πr^2
- volume of a cylinder = $\pi r^2 h$
- volume of a sphere = $\frac{4}{3}\pi r^3$
- volume of a cone = $\frac{1}{3}\pi r^2 h$

1 Look at these cross-sections. Calculate the areas.

1 30 mm 20 mm

______

2

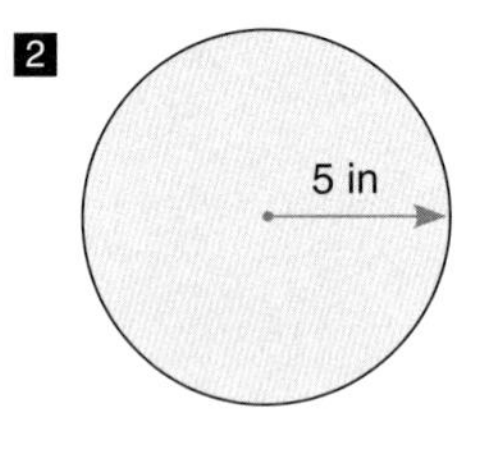

______

3

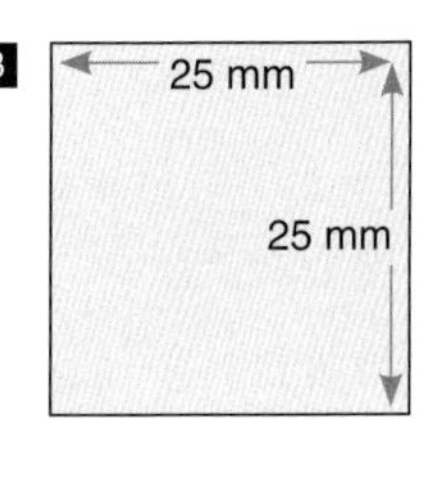

______

Language

Calculations

Note how we say calculations:

20 × 30 = 600 = *twenty times thirty is/equals 600*	= equals
πr^2 = *pi r squared*	+ plus
$2\pi r$ = *two pi r*	– minus
600 m^2 = *six hundred square metres*	/ divided by
600 m^3 = *six hundred cubic metres*	× multiplied by/times
√ 64 = 8 = *the square root of sixty-four is eight*	√ the square root of

2 Calculate these volumes. Compare your answers with a partner.

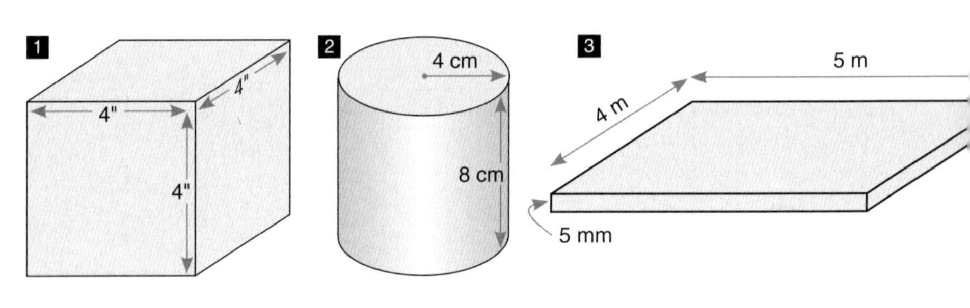

______ ______ ______

3 The answers to these calculations are incorrect. Correct the answers and then compare with a partner.

1 3 × 4 = 15
2 16 / 8 = 3
3 √ 25 = 4
4 18 – 15 = 2
5 76 + 32 = 107

Speaking

4 Work in pairs. Take turns to give each other simple calculations to do.

A: *What's the square root of 121?*
B: *11. My turn. What's 174 divided by 3?*
A: *48.*
B: *No, it's 58.*

Review

Writing **1** Write the noun (n) and adjective (adj) for each shape.

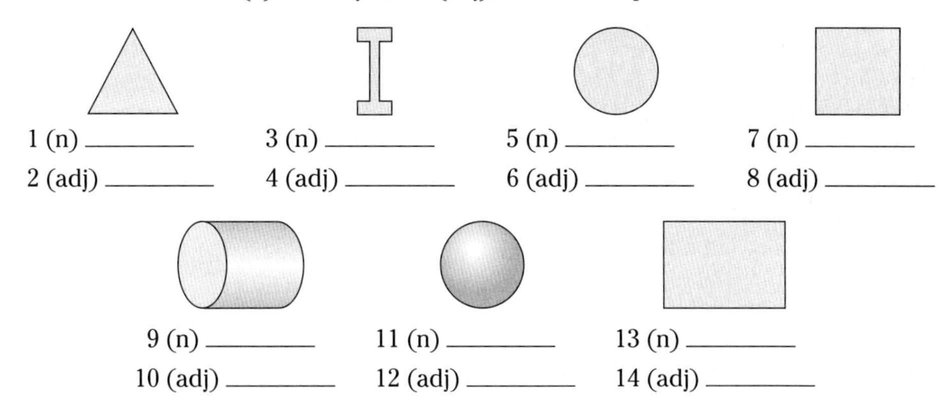

1 (n) ________ 2 (adj) ________
3 (n) ________ 4 (adj) ________
5 (n) ________ 6 (adj) ________
7 (n) ________ 8 (adj) ________
9 (n) ________ 10 (adj) ________
11 (n) ________ 12 (adj) ________
13 (n) ________ 14 (adj) ________

2 Complete this text with the words in the box.

council engineers plan staff team water

RamCo employs nine (1) ________: one general manager, one architect, two structural (2) ________, three project co-ordinators, one finance specialist and a(n) (3) ________ assistant. Susana Ramirez is the architect in charge of the Cambridge Road Hospital project. Everything is going to (4) ________, she says, except for the (5) ________ supply, which remains a problem. The solution is a new pump system, she says, but there is not enough money in the budget. The local government official, Arnold Schmidt, says that he is asking for more money from the local (6) ________ . The hospital is useless without a reliable water supply, he says.

3 Imagine you are a visitor at a contractor's office. Write answers to the receptionist's questions 1–3.

1 Can I help you?
2 Would you like coffee?
3 How long have you got?

4 Write these numbers in words.

1 2.905 2 67.98 3 0.223 4 453.608 5 14.890

5 Write these calculations in words.

1 $5 \times 6 = 30$
2 $100 / 5 = 20$
3 $\sqrt{36} = 6$
4 $5 + 3 - 1 = 7$
5 $7^2 = 7 \times 7 = 49$

6 Look at the buildings in 5 on pages 55 and 70. Write three sentences about each building. Use the information on pages 55 and 70 to help you.

8 Planning ahead

- complete a schedule
- make appointments
- talk about days, dates and time
- make comparisons
- write quantities

Planning a project

Listening **1** 47 Listen to a project manager explaining the schedule for a beam bridge and look at this diagram. Tick ✓ the four words you hear.

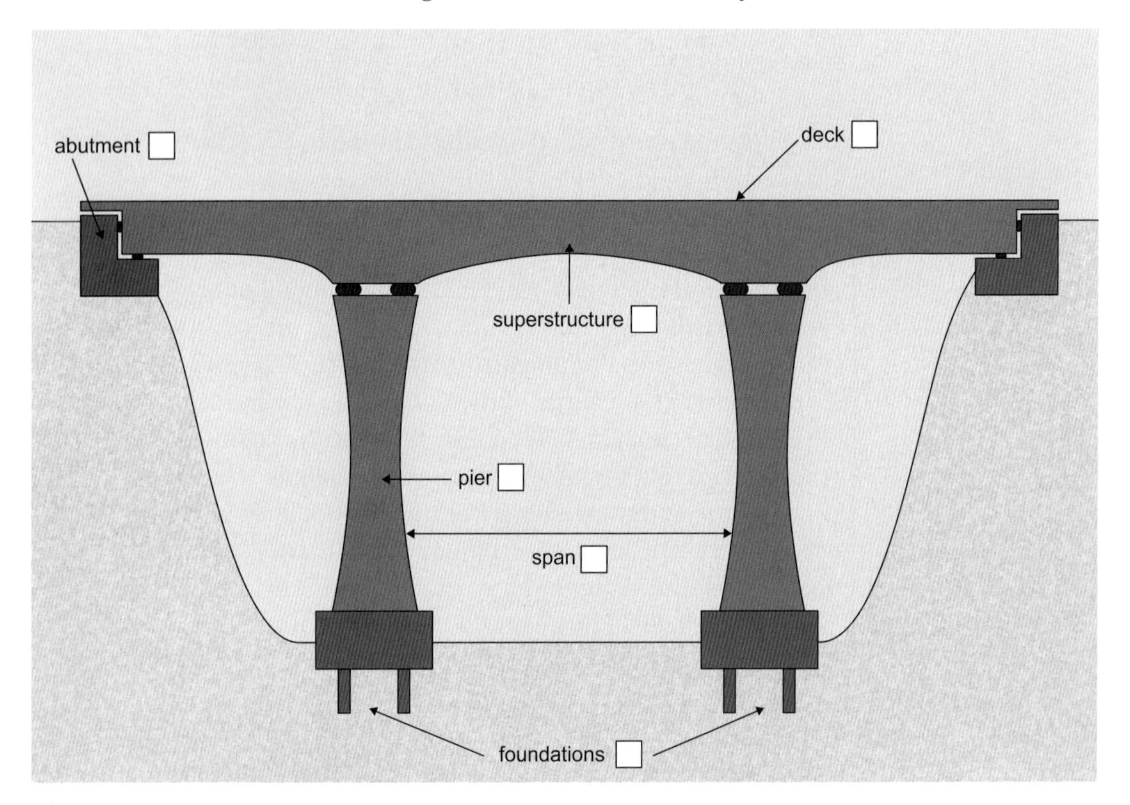

2 Are these sentences *true* (T) or *false* (F)? Correct the false sentences.

1 The deck is above the superstructure. (T / F)
2 The piers are below the foundations. (T / F)
3 The superstructure rests on the piers and abutments. (T / F)
4 The bridge has three abutments. (T / F)

Vocabulary **3** Match 1–5 to a–e to make word pairs.

1 project	a) preparations
2 beam	b) bridge
3 design	c) ceremony
4 site	d) schedule
5 opening	e) phase

Listening **4** Listen again and complete this schedule.

January
February
March
April
May
June
July
August
September
October
November
December

	Mar	Apr	May	Jun	Jul	Aug	Sept	Oct	Nov	Dec	Jan	Feb	Mar	Apr	May	Jun	Jul
Design																	
Site preparations																	
Foundations																	
Pier construction																	
Superstructure																	
Deck																	
Opening ceremony																	

5 Look at the schedule in 4 and answer these questions.

1 When will work on the foundations begin?
2 When will work on the superstructure end?
3 Will the site preparations start in June this year?
4 Will the bridge open in June next year?

Language

***Will* (future)**

We use ***will*** + the infinitive to talk about something that we think, believe or know will happen in the future.	*We'**ll** start work on the foundations at the beginning of August.* *(we'll = we will)* *I'**ll** see you next week. (I'll = I will)*	***Will** the bridge open in July? Yes, it **will**./No, it **won't** (**will not**).*

Speaking **6** Work in pairs. Student A look at the information on this page. Student B look at the information on page 71.

Student A

Look at this schedule for a bridge construction project and ask Student B for the missing information.

A: When will we do the foundations?
B: We'll start in August and we'll finish in December.
A: So, it will take five months?
B: Yes, that's right.
A: OK, what about …?

	May	Jun	Jul	Aug	Sept	Oct	Nov	Dec	Jan	Feb	Mar	Apr	May	Jun	Jul	Aug	Sept
Design																	
Site preparations																	
Foundations																	
Pier construction																	
Superstructure																	
Deck																	
Opening ceremony																	

Schedules

Listening **1** 48 Listen to five conversations and look at this calendar. Write the days of the meetings.

Monday	Tuesday	Wednesday	Thursday	Friday	Saturday	Sunday
	1	2	3	4	5	6
7	8	9	10	11	12	13
14	15	16	17	18	19	20
21	22	23	24	25	26	27
28						

1 ________ 2 ________ 3 ________ 4 ________ 5 ________

2 Write these years in figures.

1 nineteen eighty-six ______
2 eighteen oh one ______
3 twenty oh one/two thousand and one ______
4 twenty thirty-five ______
5 nineteen ninety ______
6 twenty eleven ______

3 Write these years in words.

1 1972 ____________________
2 2018 ____________________
3 2007 ____________________
4 2034 ____________________
5 2010 ____________________
6 2015 ____________________

Language

Prepositions of time

We use ***on*** with days and dates. Note: we write *22 June or 22nd June*, but we say *June the twenty-second* or *the twenty second of June*.	***on*** *Tuesday/22 June/Monday evening*	
We use ***in*** with parts of the day and longer periods of time.	***in*** *the morning/the summer*	
We use ***at*** with clock times and some expressions.	***at*** *5.15 p.m./the weekend/the moment*	
Saying years:	1998 = *nineteen ninety-eight* 2007 = *twenty oh seven/two thousand and seven*	
Making appointments:	*Are you free …* ***on*** *Tuesday?* ***on*** *Wednesday morning?* ***at*** *ten o'clock?* ***in*** *the morning?* ***next*** *week?*	*I'm free …* ***all*** *week.* ***on*** *Friday.* ***on*** *Monday evening.* ***at*** *5.30 p.m.* ***in*** *the afternoon.*
	I can't make it ***on*** *Monday.*	

Speaking **4** Work in pairs and ask and answer questions 1–6. Make a note of the answers. Then find another partner and repeat.

1 When's your birthday?
2 When was your last holiday?
3 When's your next holiday?
4 When did you last go over a bridge?
5 When did you last visit a construction site?
6 When will you retire?

Vocabulary **5** ▶ 49 Look at clocks 1–6. Listen to the times and write them in words.

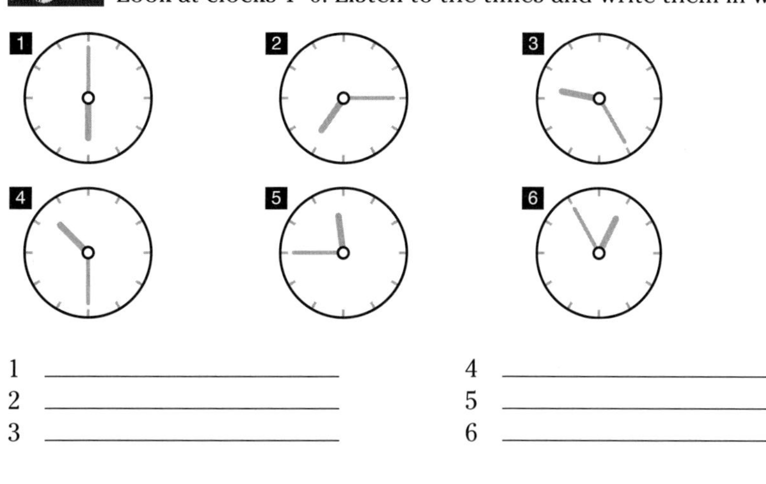

1 ______________________
2 ______________________
3 ______________________
4 ______________________
5 ______________________
6 ______________________

6 Write these times in words.

1 7.25 ______________________
2 8.45 ______________________
3 3.15 ______________________
4 2.05 ______________________
5 12.30 ______________________
6 6.10 ______________________

7 ▶ 50 Listen to seven conversations. Write the times and what is happening.

1 ______________________
2 ______________________
3 ______________________
4 ______________________
5 ______________________
6 ______________________
7 ______________________

Language

Telling the time

6.00 = six o'clock 6.05 = five past six/six oh five 6.10 = ten past six/six ten 6.15 = quarter past six/six fifteen 6.20 = twenty past six/six twenty 6.25 = twenty-five past six/six twenty-five 6.30 = half past six/six thirty 6.35 = twenty-five to seven/six thirty-five 6.40 = twenty to seven/six forty 6.45 = quarter to seven/six forty-five 6.50 = ten to seven/six fifty 6.55 = five to seven/six fifty-five **a.m.** = in the morning **p.m.** = in the afternoon/in the evening	*What's the time?/What time is it?* *It's half past seven/seven thirty.* (7.30) *It's quarter to seven/six forty-five.* (6.45) *It's five past six/six oh five.* (6.05)
Asking what time something starts:	***What time is*** *the meeting? It's* ***at*** *quarter past two/ two fifteen.* (2.15)
Making arrangements to meet:	***Are you free at*** *11 o'clock?* ***How about/What about*** *11.30?*

Speaking **8** Take out your own schedule for this week. Work in a small group. Arrange a time that suits all of you to have a two-hour meeting to discuss a new project.

Bridges

Reading **1** Read these descriptions of five bridges and match texts 1–5 to diagrams A–E.

1 In a suspension bridge, cables go from one tower to another and the deck hangs from vertical suspenders (cable or rods) attached to the main cable. ______

2 A cantilever is a beam supported at one end. In cantilever bridges, a beam balances on top of two or more other beams, or cantilever arms. ______

3 Arches are normally semicircular in shape. In this type of bridge, there are no cables or towers. ______

4 Beam bridges are the most common type of bridge. The design is very simple. The beam sits on top of two or more supports or abutments. ______

5 In a cable-stayed bridge, the cables go directly from the tower to the deck. Cable-stayed bridges can have any number of towers. ______

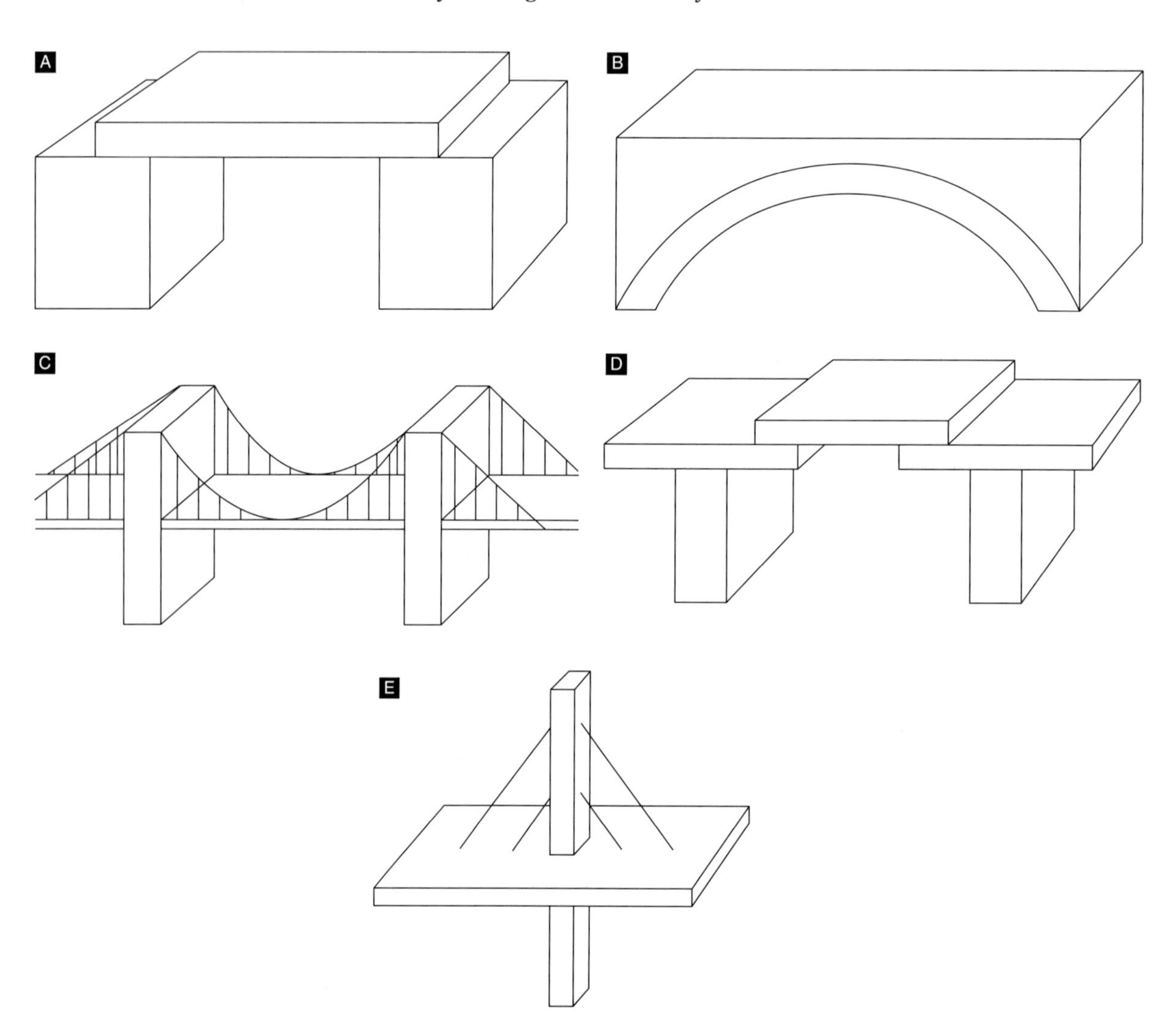

Speaking **2** Work in pairs. Cover the diagrams and the texts in 1. Together, sketch the five types of bridges in 1 and explain the differences to each other.

Reading **3** Read these texts about three cable-stayed bridges. Are sentences 1–5 *true* (T) or *false* (F)? Correct the false sentences.

The Sutong Yangtze River Bridge in China has a main span of 1,088 m. There are also side spans, making the total bridge length 8,206 m. The two highest towers in the bridge are 306 m high. The bridge opened in May 2008.

The Rion-Antirion Bridge is in Greece. Completed in August 2004, the bridge is 2,880 m long and 28 m wide. The cable-stayed deck is 2,252 m long. It has four towers, each 220 m high.

The Tatara Bridge in Japan has a total length of 1480 m, with a main span of 890 m. The deck width is 30.6 m and the towers are 220 m high. The Tatara Bridge was completed in May 1999.

1 The longest bridge is the Sutong Yangtze River Bridge. (T / F)
2 The oldest bridge is the Tatara Bridge. (T / F)
3 The Tatara Bridge is longer than the Rion-Antirion Bridge. (T / F)
4 The Rion-Antirion Bridge has the highest towers. (T / F)
5 The Sutong Yangtze River Bridge has the shortest main span. (T / F)

Language

Comparative and superlative adjectives

We use **comparative adjectives** to compare two people or things. We use **superlative adjectives** to describe one in a group of three or more people or things.	*The Rion-Antirion Bridge is long**er than** the Tatara Bridge.* ***The** old**est** bridge is the Tatara Bridge.* *long → long**er than** → **the** long**est*** *old → old**er than** → **the** old**est*** *high → high**er than** → **the** high**est*** *short → short**er than** → **the** short**est*** *new → new**er than** → **the** new**est***

4 Complete these sentences. There is more than one correct answer.

1 The Tatara Bridge is ________ than the Sutong Yangtze River Bridge.
2 The Sutong Yangtze River Bridge is ________ than the Rion-Antirion Bridge.
3 The Rion-Antirion Bridge is ________ than the Tatara Bridge and ________ than the Sutong Yangtze River Bridge.
4 The Sutong Yangtze River Bridge is the ________ .
5 The Tatara Bridge is the ________ .

Speaking **5** Work in pairs. Make comparisons about the bridges in this table.

	Completed	**Length**	**Type**	**Height** (above water)
Firth of Forth Bridge, Scotland	1890	8,296 feet	cantilever	151 feet
Golden Gate Bridge, USA	1937	8,981 feet	suspension	220 feet
Howrah Bridge, India	1943	705 m	cantilever/suspension	8.8 m

1 m = 3.28 feet

Quantities

Listening **1** 51 Listen to the conversation and answer these questions.

1 What are they talking about? ______________

2 What are they building? ______________

2 Listen again and write the quantities for 1–7.

1 brick blocks: ________
2 mortar: ________
3 concrete: ________
4 cement: ________
5 sand: ________
6 gravel: ________
7 water: ________

Language

How much/How many

We use ***how much*** to talk about quantities we can't count.	***How much*** *mortar will you need?*
We use ***how many*** to talk about quantities we can count.	***How many*** *bags of mortar will you need?*

3 *How much* or *How many?* Write the nouns in the box in the correct column. Add three more nouns to each column.

boxes bricks cement metres mortar water

How much?	How many?

Vocabulary **4** Complete these phrases.

1 a roll of ________
2 a box of ________
3 a bag of ________
4 a cup of ________
5 a packet of ________
6 a bottle of ________
7 a tin of ________
8 a flask of ________

Speaking **5** Work in pairs. Student A look at the information on this page. Student B look at the information on page 71.

Student A

You want to build a 7 m^2 single skin brick wall. Ask Student B what materials you will need, and in what quantity. Use this table to answer Student B's questions.

Brickwork (m^2): solid brick wall	Number of bricks	Number of bags of mortar
1	120	5
2	240	10
3	360	15
4	480	20
5	600	24
6	720	29
7	840	34
8	960	39
9	1080	44

Review

Writing **1** Put these phases of bridge construction in the correct order 1–7.

- [ ] foundations
- [ ] site preparations
- [ ] opening ceremony
- [1] design
- [ ] pier construction
- [ ] deck
- [ ] superstructure

2 Complete this conversation about a bridge project. Write one or two words in each gap.

A: So, when will they start the design phase?
B: In November. The whole project (1) ________ about 24 months.
A: I see. What sort of bridge (2) ________ it be?
B: It (3) ________ a simple beam bridge.
A: And how (4) ________ will it be?
B: I think the overall length will be 300 metres. But I'm not sure. (5) ________ have to check.
A: So it'll be (6) ________ than the other bridge?
B: Yes, that's right.
A: OK. How many piers will it (7) ________? Three?
B: No, the civil engineer says that two (8) ________ enough.

3 Sketch one type of bridge design. Name the bridge type and label the parts of the bridge using some of the words in the box.

abutment beam cable circular deck foundation pier rod superstructure support tower

4 Write these dates in words.

1 3 Oct 1992
2 24 Feb 2001
3 16 Mar 2010
4 12 Apr 1987

5 Write these times in words.

1 2 3 4 5 6

6 Are these questions *correct* (C) or *incorrect* (I)? Correct the mistakes.

1 How much bags of cement? (C / I)
2 How many litres of water? (C / I)
3 How much metres? (C / I)
4 How many projects? (C / I)
5 How much sand? (C / I)

7 Read this information about a bridge project and write a short text about it for your company brochure. Draw and label a diagram with the dimensions. Start like this. *We started the project in … .*

Type:	beam	**Height:**	56 m (highest point)
Materials:	steel and concrete	**Start date:**	Sept 2009
Piers:	3	**Completed:**	Nov 2010
Length:	46 m	**Location:**	northern Germany
Width:	24 m	**Client:**	government

Partner files

1 The construction industry

Finding out more

Speaking exercise 3 page 6

Student B

Read these letters to Student A. Write the letters Student A says. What do the letters mean?

PPE HV kg POL

PPE = personal protection equipment
HV = high voltage
kg = kilogram
POL = petrol, oil, lubricants

2 Trades

Trades and training

Speaking exercise 7 page 13

Student B

Read about a training institute in Dubai, United Arab Emirates (UAE) and underline the key information.

The institute is 24 years old and has over 1,000 students. The first year of training is general and includes training on basic tools and equipment, health and safety and algebra. In the second year apprentices specialise in one trade: construction electrician, painting and decorating, concrete specialist, heating, ventilation and air conditioning technician, indoor plumbing, roofing or residential glazing. The training takes three years to complete and includes on-the-job experience.

3 Heavy equipment

Controls and equipment

Speaking exercise 3 page 24

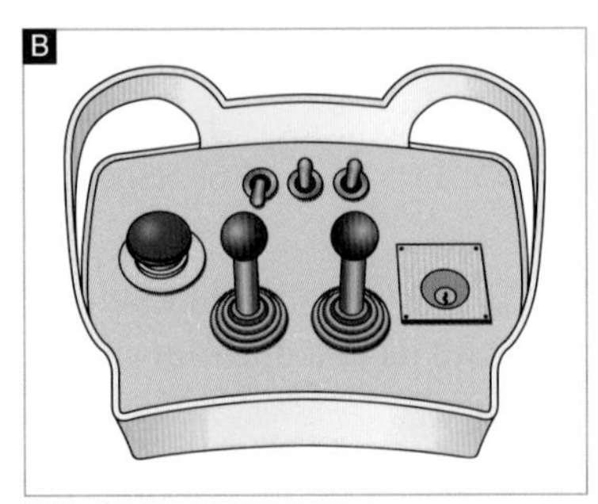

4 Building supplies

Materials

Speaking exercise 10 page 31

Student B

Read the list on the opposite page. The items are in stock in the storeroom. Answer Student A's questions. Then ask to borrow the items you need.

In stock:

- 12 m extension cable – 7
- 15 m extension cable – 10
- 5A/250V plug – 30
- 15 mm flexible metal conduit – 10 m
- 25 mm flexible metal conduit – 30 m
- 3G power cable – 25 m
- 18 mm × 30 m PVC insulating tape – 90 rolls

You have:

- spare red paint
- spray equipment (for painting)

You need to borrow:

- a paint brush

A: *Do you have three 12-metre extension cables?*
B: *Yes, we do. We have seven in stock.*
A: *What about conduits?*
B: *Yes, we have conduits. What type?*

A: *Can I borrow …?*
B: *Yes, no problem.*

4 Building supplies

Insulation

Speaking exercise 6 page 33

Student B

1 You are a customer. Read this extract from a supplier's email. Answer the phone.

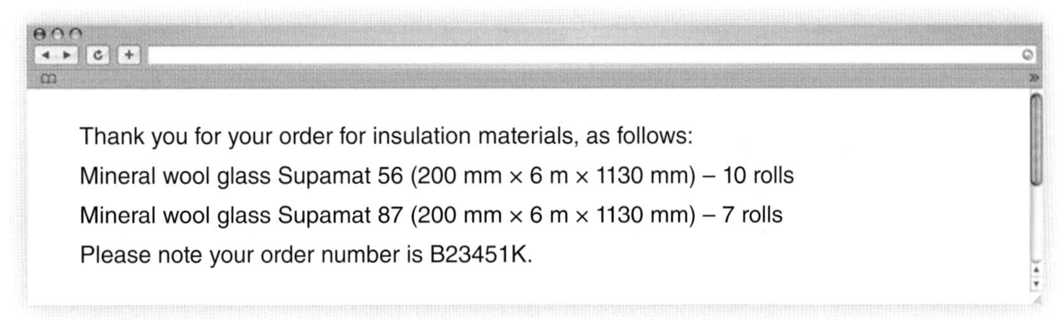

Thank you for your order for insulation materials, as follows:

Mineral wool glass Supamat 56 (200 mm × 6 m × 1130 mm) – 10 rolls

Mineral wool glass Supamat 87 (200 mm × 6 m × 1130 mm) – 7 rolls

Please note your order number is B23451K.

2 Your boss wants 17 rolls of Supamat 87, not 7. Phone the supplier and change the order.

5 On site

Directions

Speaking exercise 7 page 39

Student B

Look at these floor plans. You are at Reception. Ask Student A how to get to the following.

1 the general manager's office
2 the purchasing department
3 the toilet

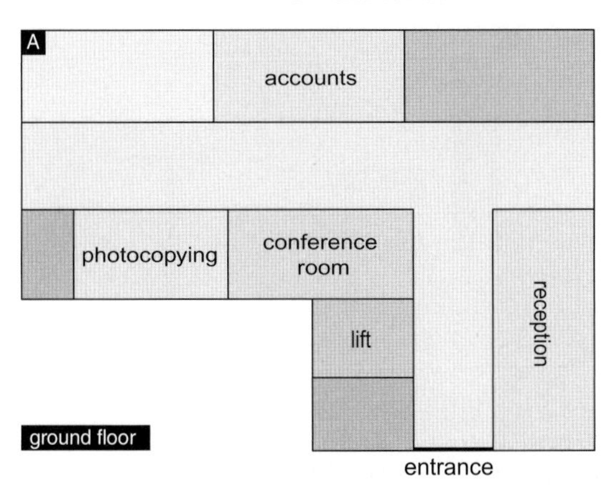

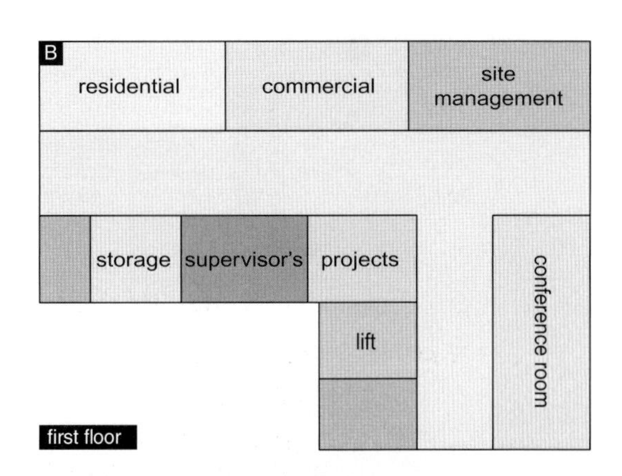

6 Health and safety

Site safety

Speaking exercise 8 page 47

Student B

Listen and make notes about the faults for vehicle GH675. Then read the list of faults for vehicle JK893 and explain them to Student A.

✓ = OK ✗ = action needed	Lights	Mirrors	Seat	Seat belt	Tyres	Fluids	Battery	Documents
GH675								
JK893	✗	✓	✓	✗	✗	✗	✓	✓

7 The contractor's office

Projects

Speaking exercise 5 page 55

Student B

Listen and take notes about Student A's building. Then look at this photo and read the information about the Burj Khalifa. Tell Student A about the building.

The Burj Khalifa

The Burj Khalifa is a skyscraper in Dubai. It is 828 metres high and has 160 floors. The total floor area is over 300,000 m^2. The building contains offices, a hotel and swimming pools, as well as 900 residential apartments. There are 24,348 windows and 2909 steps. The Burj Khalifa contains more than 330,000 m^3 of concrete and 39,000 tonnes of steel rebar.

Taipei 101
Height: (1) ______
Pendulum dimensions: (2) ______
Number of steps: (3) ______
Race record: (4) ______

7 The contractor's office

Shapes

Speaking exercise 8 page 57

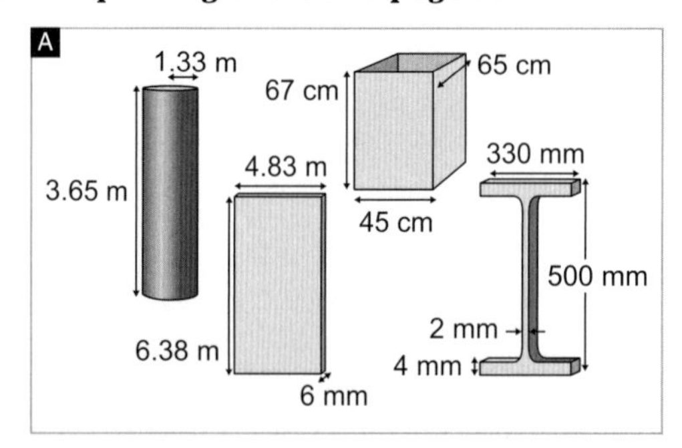

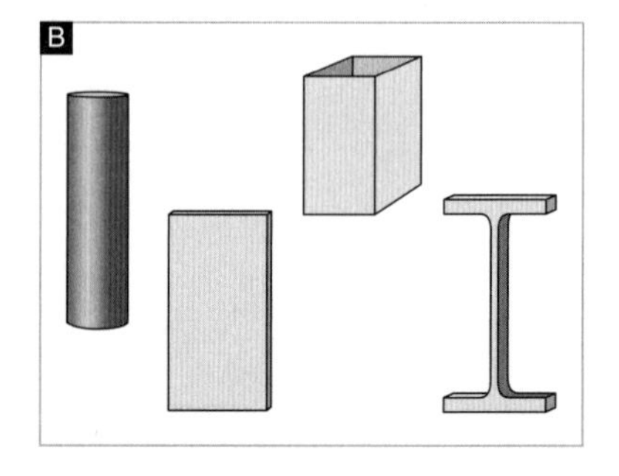

A: What are the dimensions of the rod?
B: It's 3.65 metres long, … .

A: What about the radius?
B: The radius is … .

8 Planning ahead

Planning a project

Speaking exercise 6 page 61

Student B

Look at this schedule for a bridge construction project and ask Student A for the missing information.

A: When will we do the site preparations?
B: We'll start in June and we'll finish in October.
A: So, it will take five months?
B: Yes, that's right.
A: OK, what about ... .

	May	Jun	Jul	Aug	Sept	Oct	Nov	Dec	Jan	Feb	Mar	Apr	May	Jun	Jul	Aug	Sept
Design																	
Site preparations		X	X	X	X	X											
Foundations																	
Pier construction								X	X	X							
Superstructure																	
Deck														X	X	X	
Opening ceremony																	

8 Planning ahead

Quantities

Speaking exercise 5 page 66

Student B

You want to build a 3 m^2 solid brick wall. Ask Student A what materials you will need, and in what quantity. Use this table to answer Student A's questions.

Brickwork (m^2): solid brick wall	Number of bricks	Number of bags of mortar
1	60	3
2	120	5
3	180	8
4	240	10
5	300	12
6	360	15
7	420	17
8	480	20
9	540	22

Audio script

Unit 1 The construction industry

▶ 02

1 [JT = Jun Takahashi; IR = Isabelle Roux]
JT: Hi! I'm Jun Takahashi, from the Ministry.
IR: Hi, Mr Takahashi. I'm Isabelle Roux. I'm from France. I'm the architect on this project.
JT: Ah, I'm a building inspector.
IR: Pleased to meet you.

2 [KN = Karol Nowacki; SC = Santiago Cruz]
KN: Hi! Karol Nowacki.
SC: Santiago Cruz.
KN: What do you do, Santiago?
SC: I'm a crane operator. And you?
KN: Me? I'm a roofer.

3 [KB = Kamal Boukhaled; SC = Santiago Cruz]
KB: Hi! My name is Kamal Boukhaled.
SC: Hi, Kamal. I'm Santiago.
KB: Where are you from?
SC: From Caracas, Venezuela.
KB: Ah, Caracas. A beautiful city. I come from Morocco.

4 [KB = Kamal Boukhaled; KN = Karol Nowacki; IR = Isabelle Roux]
KB: Hello. My name's Kamal Boukhaled.
KN: Hi, Kamal. I'm Karol Nowacki. And this is Isabelle Roux.
KB: Hello, Isabelle.
IR: Pleased to meet you.
KN: What do you do, Kamal?
KB: I'm a plumber.
KN: I'm a roofer. And Isabelle designs buildings.
KB: She's an architect?
IR: Yes, that's right.

▶ 03

A, H, J, K
B, C, D, E, G, P, T, V, Z
F, L, M, N, S, X, Z
I, Y
O
Q, U, W
R

▶ 04

1 A: Hello. My name's Trochowski. That's T-R-O-C-H-O-W-S-K-I.
B: First name?
A: Robert.
B: Thank you.

2 A: Carlos. Carlos del Bosque.
B: How do you spell that?
A: It's del Bosque. D-E-L. New word. B-O-S-Q-U-E.
B: Thank you.

3 A: Sasha Burgess.
B: Pardon?
A: Burgess. That's B-U-R-G-E double S.
B: Thank you.

▶ 05

1 [A = Ahmed; T = Tariq; J = Jacek]
A: Hello. I'm Ahmed. I'm the electrician. From Chestertons.
T: Chestertons, the subcontractors?
A: Yes, that's right.
T: Ah, good to see you, Ahmed. I'm Tariq. Roofer. This is Jacek. He's a roofer too.
A: Hi, Jacek.
J: Hello, Ahmed.
T: And that's Luis.
A: What does he do?
T: He's a crane operator.
A: OK.

2 [K = Kim; A = Ahmed; R = Rob; P = Pierre; L = Luis; T = Tariq]
K: OK, everybody. New people, so please say your name and your job.
A: Ahmed. Electrician. From Chestertons.
R: Rob. Labourer.
P: Pierre. Labourer.
L: Luis. Crane operator.
T: Tariq. Roofer.
K: And I'm Kim. Site manager.

3 [A = Antonio; Ah = Ahmed]
A: Hello. My name's Antonio.
Ah: Pardon?
A: Antonio.
Ah: Hi, Antonio. I'm Ahmed. Are you the new electrician?
A: No, I'm Antonio Rivaldi. Building inspector from the Ministry.
Ah: Ah, OK. Can I help you?
A: I'm looking for Kim.
Ah: Kim, the site manager? That's Kim over there.
A: Thank you.

▶ 06

1 tunnel – T-U-N-N-E-L
2 road – R-O-A-D
3 bridge – B-R-I-D-G-E
4 house – H-O-U-S-E
5 school – S-C-H-O-O-L
6 hospital – H-O-S-P-I-T-A-L
7 apartment – A-P-A-R-T-M-E-N-T
8 office block – O-F-F-I-C-E B-L-O-C-K

▶ 07

1 A: I'm looking for the site manager.
B: Are you from the school?
A: Yes, that's right.

2 A: I'm the crane operator on the new bridge.
B: Pleased to meet you.

3 A: What does he do?
B: He's an architect. He designs apartments.

4 A: That's Henrietta Samson. She works for the Ministry. She inspects office blocks.
B: Ah, I see. Thank you.

5 A: Who's that?
B: That's Ken. He's a labourer on the tunnel project.

6 A: I'm looking for Salim.
B: Salim?
A: Yes, he's in charge of the roofers at the hospital.

08

A: Can you tell me about the house?
B: Yes, of course. The house has two floors. We have a kitchen, two bathrooms and two bedrooms. The kitchen opens out into a family area and a dining area. We also have a porch.
A: Did you say two bathrooms?
B: Yes, that's right. And two bedrooms.
A: OK. What about the garden?

Unit 2 Trades

09

Hi! My name's Sam Smith. I'm an electrician by trade. I work on building sites. I'm also an instructor at a vocational school. Today I want to talk about trades. Trades normally have three stages. The first stage is apprentice. Apprentices are supervised at work and learn on the job. Most apprentices also attend vocational school and get a qualification. The second stage is journeyman. Journeymen work unsupervised. A master is the third stage. Masters supervise other workers, and also train apprentices.

10

1 thirteen 2 forty 3 sixty 4 nine

11

1 fifty-six, thirty-four, eighty-nine, sixty-three, seventy-six, twenty-one
2 thirteen, thirty, fourteen, forty, sixteen, sixty

12

The office block has six floors. Each floor has twenty-two rooms. Each room has two windows and a door, so there are forty-four windows per floor and twenty-two doors. Each window is 1 m 20 by 80 cm. Each room is 32 m^2.

13

[L= Lenny, construction worker; F = Foreman; M = Mickey, apprentice; J = Jeff, apprentice; S = Sam, apprentice]

1 L: Where are the base plates? On the truck too?
F: No, they're behind the truck.
L: OK, thanks.

2 L: I need a hammer. For the base plate nails.
M: My hammer is in the toolbox.
L: Where is it?
M: The toolbox? It's in front of the truck.
L: Thanks.

3 J: Where are the coupling pins? And the locking pins?
F: In a box, behind the truck, next to the base plates. Ask Lenny.
J: Thanks.

4 S: Where are the jacks?
F: Behind the truck. Between the base plates and the box of pins.
S: OK, thanks.

5 F: Where's my flask?
All: Under the truck.
F: OK, thanks.

14

[F = Foreman; M = Mickey, apprentice]
F: So, Mickey. Is Mickey short for Michael?
M: No, it's a nickname. It's short for Mickey Mouse. I have big ears.
F: Ah! I see. What's your real name?
M: Ken. Ken Chambers.
F: Where are you from?
M: Manchester.
F: Manchester? That's a long way from here. Do you live in Manchester?
M: No, I don't. I live in Leeds.
F: Ah! OK. Which college do you go to?
M: Leeds Construction.
F: Is that near the centre?
M: Yes. Near the hospital.
F: What trade?
M: I'm a plumber.
F: And how old are you?
M: I'm nineteen. Almost twenty. My birthday is on Thursday.
F: Did you say Thursday? That's interesting.
M: Why?
F: My birthday is on Thursday too. Coffee?
M: Yes, please. Thanks.

15

[J = Jeff, apprentice; M = Mickey, apprentice]
J: When's the party, Mickey?
M: Saturday.
J: What time?
M: Eight o'clock.
J: Where?
M: At my place.
J: What's the address?
M: Sixteen, Conworth Road.
J: Is that C-O-N-W-O-R-T-H?
M: Yes, that's right.
J: OK. Oh, what's your telephone number, in case there's a problem?
M: It's 564362.
J: Did you say 362 or 363?
M: 362.
J: Thanks. See you on Saturday.
M: Great!

Unit 3 Heavy equipment

16

1 A: What's in the crate?
B: A rebar cutter.
A: A what?
B: A rebar cutter. You know, to cut rebar.
A: Ah, OK.

2 A: What's in the box?
B: The label says MIG welding equipment. Hang on. Ah, it's welding wire.

3 A: What's on the pallet?
B: It looks like sheets of glass.
A: OK.

17

1 A: What's on the flatbed, under the sheeting?
B: Rebar. Lots of rebar.
A: What are you doing?
B: I'm phoning the suppliers. We don't need rebar. Hello? Hello? Is that Harrisons? We have a problem. Your man is unloading rebar in our car park. We don't need rebar. We don't use rebar. Why? I don't know why! OK. Uh-huh. Thank you.
A: What's happening?
B: It's a mistake. He's phoning his driver now.

2 A: Good morning.
B: Morning.
A: I have a delivery for the site carpenter, Abdul Karim.
B: Ah, yes. He's waiting for the timber. Flooring timber, right?
A: No, roofing timber.
B: Oh! Park over there, please. I think we have a problem.

3 A: Hello. I'm looking for the site manager.
B: Sure. I'm the site manager. Janek Krol. What's up?
A: Hi! I'm Marc Martin, from Martin's Aggregates.
B: Hello. Good to see you. We are waiting for your sand.
A: Yes, well, the sand is coming – in about two hours.
B: Two hours? Why? I need the sand now.
A: I'm sorry. We're waiting for the driver.
B: What?
A: The driver's running late. I'm really sorry.

18

Crane operators use different controls to raise and lower the boom, rotate the cab, extend and retract the boom, wind and unwind the winch and control other equipment. This operator has two joysticks. One controls left-to-right movement of the boom and the other controls forward and backward movement. The operator uses the foot pedals to retract or extend the boom.

19

1 A: What's this? A remote control?
B: It's a remote control. That's right.

2 A: What's this for?
B: It's for extending the boom.

3 A: What does this do?
B: It starts the motor.

4 A: How do I extend the boom?
B: Extend it? You use the pedal.

5 A: How do I lower the boom?
B: Lower it? You move the joystick.

6 A: What's this switch for? Is it the power switch?
B: Yes, that's the power switch.

20

1 A: Did you say turn the key?
B: Yes, that's right.
A: Clockwise or anticlockwise?
B: Clockwise.
A: Thanks.

2 A: What do I do next?
B: Press the start button.
A: OK. Which one is the start button?
B: It's the green one, on the left.
A: Thank you.

3 A: How do I start the engine?
B: Press the green button and turn the key.
A: And how do I stop it?
B: Switch off? Press the big red button here.
A: Thanks.

21

1 A: Where's the sand?
B: I think it's on the way.
A: I hope so.

2 A: Where are the base plates?
B: I'm sure they're in the truck.
A: Ah, OK. That makes sense.

3 A: I think the boom is too high.
B: Ah, yes, you're right. Use the radio and speak to the operator.
A: OK. Good idea.

4 A: I think the concrete is too hard.
B: I don't think so. It looks OK to me.
A: Are you sure?
B: OK, go and ask Jim.
A: Will do.

5 A: Where's your hard hat?
B: Over there. Why?
A: Go and get it. You must wear a hard hat in this area.
B: OK. Here it is.

6 A: We have a problem. There's a hole in the hopper.
B: John's in the house. He's a welder. Ask him to fix it.
A: Good idea. Thanks.
B: You're welcome.

7 A: Don't touch the flask.
B: Why? Is it yours?
A: No, it's Norman's.
B: Fair enough.

Unit 4 Building supplies

22

[ES = Ernest Smith; JJ = Jenny Jones]
ES: Smith and Sons Construction Supplies. Customer services, Ernest Smith speaking. Can I help you?
JJ: Hello, this is Jenny Jones from Apex Building. I'd like to place an order, please.
ES: Certainly. One moment, please. OK, go ahead.
JJ: My customer number is 25673929.
ES: 25673929. Thank you.
JJ: I'd like to order some chipboard, please. That's item number AJ437 and I'd like ten pieces, please.
ES: OK, so that's ten pieces of AJ437.

JJ: Yes. I'd also like some plywood, item numbers HB392, four pieces, and HB396, nine pieces.
ES: HB392, four pieces, and HB396, nine pieces.
JJ: Yes, that's right.
ES: Anything else?
JJ: Yes, one more thing. I'd like some timber, please. Item number XP6754. Is it in stock?
ES: Just one moment. I'll check.
JJ: Thank you.
ES: No, I'm sorry. We're out of stock. We expect some next week.
JJ: No problem.
ES: OK, thank you. Is that for delivery or pick-up?
JJ: Pick-up, please. Is tomorrow morning OK?
ES: Yes, that's fine. So that's for pick-up on the 8th of July. Thank you very much.
JJ: Thank you.
ES: Just one more thing. Your order number is GGC33471. I'll send you an email to confirm.
JJ: That's great. Thank you. Goodbye.
ES: Thank you. Bye.

23

[ES = Ernest Smith; JJ = Jenny Jones]
ES: Smith and Sons Construction Supplies. Customer services, Ernest Smith speaking.
JJ: Hello, this is Jenny Jones from Apex Building. I'd like to change an order, please.
ES: Certainly. Just a moment, please. OK, go ahead.
JJ: My customer number is 25673929. The order number is GGC33471.
ES: OK. What's the change?
JJ: The item number is HB392, that's plywood. I ordered four pieces but we now need eight pieces.
ES: OK, so change the order to eight pieces?
JJ: Yes, that's right.
ES: Anything else?
JJ: No, that's all. Thank you.
ES: OK, thank you. Goodbye.
JJ: Goodbye.

24

[I = Isaac; A = Alex]
I: Hi, Alex. How's it going?
A: Hi, Isaac. Good, thanks. And you?
I: Yes, all good. Alex, I need some electrical supplies. Do you have a spare roll of insulating tape in your toolbox?
A: Let's see. Yes, I do. Here you are.
I: Thank you very much. That's great.
A: You're welcome.
I: Do you have an extension cable?
A: Yes, I think I do.
I: I need fifteen metres.
A: Fifteen metres? I only have five metres.
I: Oh, that's fine for now, thanks. One last thing. Can I borrow your drill?
A: No, I'm sorry. It's broken.
I: OK, I'll ask Tom. Thanks, anyway.
A: No problem.

25

A: Can you tell me about wall insulation?
B: Sure. There are two types of wall insulation: cavity and solid. Both types provide thermal and acoustic insulation.
A: What's the difference?
B: Let me explain. Sometimes walls are solid, so the insulation is on the outside of the wall. This is solid wall insulation.

26

A: And cavity wall insulation?
B: Sometimes walls have two parts: an inner wall and an outer wall. Cavity wall insulation means that the insulation material is inside the wall.
A: Ah, OK. So solid wall is outside and cavity wall is inside?
B: Yes, exactly.
A: OK, I understand. And what types of insulation do you use for cavity wall insulation?
B: Our company uses three types of cavity wall insulation to fill the gap: foam, mineral wool, or polystyrene beads.
A: What about pipes?
B: For pipes, we normally use felt tape or foam tubing.
A: I see. Thank you.

27

A: Let's check the list.
B: OK. First question. How's the concrete?
A: The concrete on the second floor is still liquid.
B: What about the first floor?
A: The concrete on the first floor is solid.
B: That's good. What about the paint?
A: The paint is OK. It's all dry.
B: Yes, today was nice and hot. Perfect for paint.
A: Is the concrete aggregate all right?
B: No, it's too coarse.
A: I'll speak to the supplier.
B: Thanks.
A: And the scaffolding. Is it up?
B: No, the scaffolding is heavy and the ground is too soft. We need timber to make mudsills.
A: OK.
B: Oh, and one last thing. You know the new toolboxes?
A: Yes.
B: They're too small.
A: No way!

Unit 5 On site

28

1 I examine plans and check buildings. I test electrical and plumbing systems, and make sure that buildings are safe. I'm a building inspector.
2 I work on building sites. I install or replace roofing systems. Sometimes I erect scaffolding. I'm a roofer.
3 I design buildings. I work in an office. I co-ordinate construction drawings and specifications from different subcontractors. I'm an architect.
4 I work on building sites. I lift equipment and materials. I also maintain my crane. I'm a crane operator.
5 I work in buildings. I install water pipes and drainage systems. I'm a plumber.

29

[D = Driver; P = Pedestrian]

D: Excuse me, can you tell me where Mill Street is? I'm looking for the construction site.
P: Mill Street?
D: Yes, that's right. The Mill Street construction site.
P: Ah, yes, of course. From here, go to the roundabout.
D: The roundabout. OK.
P: Take the first exit. Then drive past the hospital, under the railway bridge and through the tunnel.
D: OK, so, first exit, past the hospital, under the railway bridge and through the tunnel.
P: Yes, that's right. Mill Street is the second street on the left after the tunnel. You can't miss the entrance to the construction site. There's a big sign next to the gate.
D: The second street on the left. Thank you.
P: You're welcome.

30

1 The hospital? No problem. Go down to the roundabout and turn right. The hospital is on your right.
2 Sam's Paint Shop? Go straight over the roundabout and take the first left. Then take the second right. Sam's Paint Shop is on your right. You can't miss it.
3 The city hall? Go to the roundabout. Turn left and then go all the way to the T-junction. Turn right. The city hall is on your right.

31

[V = Visitor; C = Construction worker]

V: Hi, can you tell me where the site manager's office is, please? I have some paperwork for him.
C: Yes, of course. You see the tower crane? Over there?
V: Yes.
C: Drive past the crane. Go down a ramp and follow the signs to the car park. You can't miss it.
V: OK.
C: From the car park you'll see a fence, and behind the fence is a row of portable cabins. The site manager's office is the second from the left – the blue one.
V: Thank you.

32

1 A: More snow on the way?
B: I hope not. We're working on the roof at the moment.
2 A: Hmm. Look, lots of clouds are coming in.
B: Yes, but no rain was forecast for today.
A: Ah, good.
3 A: This wind is getting stronger.
B: Yes. That's why we're tying down the sheeting on the timber. We don't want it to blow away.
A: Good idea.
4 A: I hate this rain! And the cold.
B: Me too. Mind the puddle!
A: Urgh! I really hate this rain.
5 A: It's very hot today.
B: Yes. It's at least forty degrees.
A: It feels like forty-five.
B: And the sun is so bright. I need my sunglasses.
A: And sun cream. Sunburn is a real problem.
B: So is dehydration. We're drinking a lot of water.
6 A: Looks like there's a storm coming. Shall I call the crane operator down?
B: No, he's all right in his cab. But get the workers away from the hopper in case there's lightning.
A: OK.

33

1 A: How's it going?
B: Well, we can't work on the roof at the moment.
A: Why not?
B: Because of the rain. It's too dangerous.
A: Ah, yes, OK.
2 A: What's the weather like?
B: It's very cold. There's lots of snow.
A: Are there any delays?
B: Yes. The trucks can't get to the site. There's just too much snow. We're clearing it at the moment.
A: OK, good.
3 A: Is that a sand storm coming in?
B: Yes, I think so.
A: OK. Call the men in. We can't work outside in this.
B: OK.
4 A: What's up?
B: The sheeting is blowing away.
A: What sheeting? The sheeting on the scaffolding?
B: Yes, because of the wind. It's too strong.
A: Can you tie it down?
B: It's too late, I think.
5 A: Is everything OK?
B: No, one man is injured. He has a broken arm.
A: What? How? Because of the rain?
B: No, because of the ice. There's ice on the ladders. It's very cold here. It's below zero.

Unit 6 Health and safety

34

1 A: What's that sound?
B: Fork lift trucks. We're moving some pallets.
A: Oh, OK.
2 A: The roofers are working today. So be careful around the building. They often drop things.
B: OK. Thanks.
3 A: We are erecting scaffolding today. So be careful.
B: OK.
4 A: It's cold today.
B: Yes. There's ice on the ground. I put up a sign.
5 A: We're using cranes today, so be careful.
B: OK.
6 A: Careful when you move the cranes today. There are electrical cables everywhere.
B: OK. Thanks.

7 A: It's a construction site, so there's a lot of debris on the ground.
B: OK, thanks. I'll be careful.

8 A: We had a break-in last week.
B: Is that why we have guard dogs now?
A: Yes, exactly.

35

A: OK, let's go through the checklist. Today is ...?
B: Tuesday.
A: OK. What's the vehicle number?
B: BH324.
A: BH324. How are the lights?
B: They're all fine.
A: And the brake lights, too?
B: Yes. They're all OK.
A: And what about the mirrors?
B: One is broken.
A: Hmm, OK. What about the seat and seat belt?
B: Both are OK.
A: And the tyres?
B: Yes, they're all good. The front right looks a little worn, though.
A: No, it's OK. Fluids?
B: They're all full. But there's a battery leak.
A: A leak?
B: Yes. There's liquid under the battery. And there's a crack.
A: Let's see. Yes, it's cracked. OK, I'll make a note of that.
B: Is that it?
A: No, what about the documents?
B: Erm, there are no documents. They're missing.
A: Hmm, OK. Right.

36

1 A: Can I help you?
B: Hello, doctor. Yes, please. I think I sprained my ankle yesterday. I tripped on some debris on the building site.
A: Let's have a look. Yes, it's very swollen. You need an X-ray.

2 A: What's up?
B: It's not me. It's Ahmed. He fell off the scaffolding. He broke his arm.
A: I'll call an ambulance!
B: Yes, hurry!

3 A: What's the matter?
B: He burnt his knee. He was welding.
A: Ouch!

4 A: I hurt my back because the wheelbarrow was too heavy. Can I go and see the doctor?
B: Of course. Let me know what he says.

5 A: That glass is sharp. I cut my finger.
B: Be careful! You're dripping blood on me.
A: Sorry! Any idea where the first aid kit is?
B: In the site manager's office.
A: Thanks.
B: And next time, wear gloves.

6 A: What happened?
B: The pallet crushed his hand.
A: How?
B: It fell off the truck.

37

First I washed my hands. Then I put on disposable gloves and cleaned the cut. I didn't have water, so I used disinfectant. Then I dried the cut with cotton wool and covered it with a plaster. And that was it, all finished.

38

[S = Susan, health and safety officer; J = John, medical supplier]

S: Hello. John?
J: Hi, Susan. How's it going?
S: Great, thanks. Listen, I need some medical supplies for the first aid kit. It's almost empty.
J: OK, no problem. What do you need?
S: Let's see, two rolls of tape, one tube of antiseptic cream, three boxes of plasters and a couple of packets of cotton wool. Is that OK?
J: Sure. I'll put them at reception. You can pick them up tomorrow.
S: Thanks. Oh, and one more thing: I also need a bottle of disinfectant, please.
J: OK, I've got that. Anything else?
S: No, that's it. Thanks, John.
J: You're welcome. Anytime. Take care now.
S: You too. Bye.
J: Bye.

39

A: I hear we have a new system for waste disposal.
B: Yes, that's right. There's a notice outside the manager's office.
A: OK, let's see. Manuals – they go in packaging, right?
B: Yes.
A: And left-over food is easy – biohazard.
B: Yes.
A: Steel pipe is metal. Hmm, paint tins. Where do old paint tins go? In the metal skip?
B: No, the metal skip is for clean metal only. Use the skip with the orange label for paint tins.
A: Ah, OK. What about old sheeting? It's polythene, I think. Does it go in packaging?
B: No, packaging is only for paper and cardboard. Use the mixed skip.
A: OK. And the tarmac from the old road? I guess that's inert, right?
B: No, wrong again. It's hazardous.
A: Hmm, OK. Wood is easy. That's green, right?
B: Only untreated wood goes in green. Painted wood is hazardous.
A: OK, thanks.
B: You're welcome.

Unit 7 The contractor's office

40

[AS = Arnold Schmidt; SR = Susana Ramirez; R = Receptionist]

1 AS: Hello. My name's Arnold Schmidt. I'm from the Council. I'm here to see Susana Ramirez.
R: Ah, yes. One moment, please. She's expecting you.

2 SR: Hello. I'm Susana Ramirez. I'm the general manager of RamCo. I'm also the project

manager in charge of the Cambridge Road Hospital project. You must be Mr Schmidt.
AS: Yes, that's right. Pleased to meet you.

3 SR: Before we start, would you like coffee?
AS: Yes, please. With milk and one sugar, please.

4 SR: OK. How about if I introduce you to the team first? Then we can look at the designs and you can ask any questions you have.
AS: That sounds perfect.

5 SR: How long have we got?
AS: I have to leave at 11.30. So we've got about an hour.

41

[SR = Susana Ramirez; RM = Rowena Murphy; AS = Arnold Schmidt; TM = Thomas McNamara; JZ = Julita Zielinski; NO = Nasim Orgun]
SR: So, this is Rowena Murphy.
RM: Pleased to meet you.
AS: What do you do here, Rowena?
RM: I'm a Structural Engineer. I do all the calculations to make sure the buildings stay up.
AS: I see.
SR: And this is Thomas McNamara. He's a student working with us for six months. He's working on a residential project at the moment – a block of flats in the centre of town. An unusual feature is the garden on the roof.
AS: How do you do?
TM: Pleased to meet you.
AS: What are you studying, Thomas?
TM: Civil engineering. I hope to graduate next year.
AS: Good luck.
TM: Thanks.
SR: And this is Julita Zielinski. She's our Team Assistant. She's in charge of the staff schedule, so she makes sure we are all in the right place at the right time.
AS: Hello, Julita.
JZ: Hello.
SR: Julita's also the only one who knows how to fix the photocopier.
AS: Ah.
SR: This is Nasim Orgun, our Bookkeeper. She looks after our finances.
AS: Hi!
NO: Hello.
SR: Erm. And that's it. We have four more employees, but they're all out of the office at the moment. One is on holiday and the others are either visiting clients or on site.
AS: OK.

42

[AS = Arnold Schmidt; SR = Susana Ramirez]
SR: This is Block A. This is all new. The basic design is arcade structure. This means that there's a central passage down the middle of the block, with rooms on each side. The passage is glass covered.
AS: How long is the passage?
SR: The passage is 250 m long and 16 m wide, so it has an area of 4000 m^2. There are shops and other amenities on each side, on the ground floor.
AS: Sorry. Did you say the length is 250 m?
SR: Yes, that's right.
AS: Thank you. What amenities do you mean?
SR: Let's see. We have two banks, a gift shop, two cafés, a restaurant, a bookshop, a post office, a toy shop. Oh, and a fruit shop.
AS: And the roof? How high is it?
SR: The height from the top of the roof to the ground is 25 m. There are five floors in the building. As I said, the passage is glass and the rest of the building has a trussed roof with terracotta tiles.

43

[AS = Arnold Schmidt; SR = Susana Ramirez]

1 SR: These are the doors we plan to use in Block A. They're all GRP.
AS: Excuse me – GRP?
SR: Glass reinforced polyester. It's very easy to clean and it doesn't have the same problems that wooden or steel doors have. For example, wood rots and metal rusts.
AS: I see.
SR: We're using a local manufacturer as the main supplier, Hingewell Doors.
AS: Hingewell Doors? Yes, I know the owner. That's good.

2 AS: What about the water supply? I understand there are some problems.
SR: Yes, the water supply is a little difficult due to the location. There are problems with the water pressure. It's not reliable. Sometimes it's too high and sometimes it's too low.
AS: I see.

3 AS: What about parking?
SR: Yes, parking is difficult in this part of town. We have plans for a multi-storey car park.
AS: Isn't that expensive?
SR: Yes, it is. But there's no other solution. We need to have parking for visitors.
AS: Yes, of course.

44

A The room is rectangular.
B The truss is triangular.
C The rod is circular.
D The damper is spherical.
E The girder is I-shaped.
F The beam is square.
G The can is cylindrical.

45

1	cylinder	cylindrical
2	rectangle	rectangular
3	triangle	triangular
4	circle	circular

46

A: Let's do the I-shaped cross-section first. All dimensions are in inches. The flange width is 12.855 and the flange thickness is 0.960.
B: 12.855 and 0.960. Right.
A: The web thickness is 0.605.
B: OK.
A: The beam height is 24.48 and the area is 38.5 in^2.
B: 38.5. OK.
A: Now, the standard channel cross-section. Again, all dimensions are in inches. The depth is 15, the width

is 3.520, the web thickness is 0.520 and the area is 11.8 in^2.
B: Slow down, please. Can you read them again?
A: Sure. Depth 15, width 3.520, web thickness 0.520 and the area is 11.8 in^2.
B: OK, thanks.
A: And the last one is the rod. This time the dimensions are in metric. The radius is 13 mm and the length is 3 m.
B: 13 mm and 3 m. OK, great. Thanks.

Unit 8 Planning ahead

47

I'd like to explain the project schedule for the Highway 473 beam bridge. As you can see from the slide, the design phase will take from March to June. At the end of May we'll begin the site preparations, which will take four months. At the beginning of August we'll start work on the foundations. These will take until the beginning of November. In November we'll start work on the piers, which will take around three months. In the middle of February we'll start work on the superstructure, and in June we'll lay the deck. The opening ceremony will be in July next year.

48

1 A: How about Wednesday the 23rd? For the project meeting, I mean?
B: Yes, that's fine with me. I'm free all day.

2 A: Let's meet on Tuesday.
B: The 8th?
A: No, the 15th. I can't make the 8th. I have to visit a supplier.
B: OK, no problem.

3 A: We need to meet next week. How about the 24th or 25th?
B: The 24th is no good. I have another meeting that day, about the hospital project.
A: Ah, yes. Then we'll have to meet on the 25th.
B: OK. It's in the diary.

4 A: Are you free on Friday the 11th?
B: I'm sorry, Friday is full. How about the 14th?
A: Yes, that's OK. I'll be there in the afternoon.
B: OK.

5 A: How about the 28th?
B: I'm sorry. The 28th is no good. I have a project meeting.
A: OK. How about the 27th?
B: The 27th is full, too. But I'm free on the 26th.
A: The 26th? Yes, that's fine with me, too. Great.

49

1 six o'clock
2 seven fifteen or quarter past seven
3 nine twenty-five or twenty-five past nine
4 ten thirty or half past ten
5 eleven forty-five or quarter to twelve
6 twelve fifty-five or five to one

50

1 A: Hi! Rebecca. The client will be here at nine o'clock. A Ms Gorski – Anita Gorski.
B: OK, thanks.

2 A: Hi! Rebecca. The meeting with the subcontractors is now at nine fifteen.
B: OK, that's no problem.

3 A: What time is it?
B: It's three twenty-five.
A: And when will the concrete be here?
B: Between four and four thirty.
A: Hmm. We'll have to hurry.
B: Yes.

4 A: What's the time?
B: I don't know. About five thirty maybe?
A: He's late. He said five fifteen.
B: Who said five fifteen?
A: The contractor. Mr Perez.
B: I see.

5 A: What time is the project meeting?
B: It starts at 10 a.m. and finishes at around 5 p.m.
A: Seven hours?
B: Yes.

6 A: How about nine forty-five to talk about the rebar delivery?
B: No, I'm sorry. I can't make that. How about half past ten?
A: Yes, half past ten is fine.

7 A: Are you free at quarter to four? Mr Sanchez will be here.
B: Yes, of course. No problem.

51

A: Can we talk about the quantities now?
B: Sure.
A: What will we need? How many blocks?
B: We'll have ten square metres of brickwork in the wall, so we'll need 100 blocks. It's roughly ten blocks per square metre.
A: OK. And how much mortar will we need?
B: Let's see. We calculate two bags per square metre, so that's ...
A: Twenty bags.
B: Yes, exactly.
A: OK, that's fine. What about the path?
B: The path will be concrete. We'll need about one cubic metre of concrete. So that will be eight bags of cement, twenty-five bags of sand, forty-five bags of gravel and, of course, water.
A: Sorry, how many bags of gravel did you say?
B: Forty-five. And twenty-five bags of sand.
A: OK. And how much water will we need?
B: 150 litres will be enough.
A: OK, that won't be a problem.

Pearson Education Limited
Edinburgh Gate
Harlow
Essex CM20 2JE
England
and Associated Companies throughout the world.

www.pearsonelt.com

First published 2012

ISBN: 978-1-4082-6991-6

Set in ITC Cheltenham Book
Printed by Graficas Estella, Spain

Acknowledgements
The publishers and author would like to thank the following people and institutions for their feedback and comments during the development of the material:

Edward Halton, UAE; Julie Cordell-Szczurek, Germany; Pamela Heath, Canada; Sotirios Koutskoukos, UK; Tony Higgins, UK

The publishers would like to thank the following for their kind permission to reproduce their photographs:

(Key: b-bottom; c-centre; l-left; r-right; t-top)

4 Alamy Images: TongRo Image Stock (A). **Getty Images:** Marc Romanelli (C). **Photolibrary.com:** Jim Toomey / age fotostock (D). **SuperStock:** Tetra Images (E); Stockbroker (B). **5 Shutterstock.com:** Katy89. **6 Shutterstock.com:** Marko Marcello. **8 Fotolia.com:** gaelj (3). **Pearson Education Ltd:** Jules Selmes (7); John Foxx Images and Images 4 Communication (2). **Shutterstock.com:** Stephen Mahar (6); ruzanna (1); QQ7 (8); KK Art and Photography (5); Andy Dean Photography (4). **12 Construction Photography:** Ray Hardinge (7). **Fotolia.com:** thijimcox (3); Lisa F. Young (8); Bogdan Vasilescu (6). **Pearson Education Ltd:** Ben Nicholson (2). **Shutterstock.com:** Yellowj (4); sculpies (5); Lisa F. Young (1). **13 DK Images:** Andy Crawford (A). **Pearson Education Ltd:** Gareth Boden (B). **14 Fotolia.com:** Sirena Designs (F); Roman Millert (A); Rafal Olechowski (B). **Pearson Education Ltd:** Image Source (E); Gareth Boden (D). **Shutterstock.com:** SVLuma (C). **21 Shutterstock.com:** Alberto Tirado. **22 Shutterstock.com:** Rob Kints (l); Lusoimages (r). **23 Photolibrary.com:** Jim Toomey / age fotostock.**25 Fotolia.com:** StockHouse (B); skaljac (A). **Shutterstock.com:** Timothy Large (F); Orange Line Media (D); Kzenon (E); Dr Ajay Kumar Singh (C). **26 Alamy Images:** Blend Images. **28 Alamy Images:** Golden Pixels LLC (B). **Art Directors and TRIP Photo Library:** Helene Rogers (D). **Fotolia.com:** Kzenon (E); Aaron Kohr (F). **Shutterstock.com:** photogen (C); GQ (A). **29 Fotolia.com:** kosoff (A); Ken Ng (I); Joe Gough (H); dbvirago (F). **Pearson Education Ltd:** Trevor Clifford (E). **Shutterstock.com:** Sue Ashe (D); olmarmar (G); Max Blain (C); L F File (K); Isabella Pfenninger (B); Evok20 (J). **30 Fotolia.com:** Fatbob. **31 Fotolia.com:** WINIKI (A); Oleksandr Dorokhov (C); Brian Weed (B). **33 Photolibrary.com:** Blend Images (A). **Shutterstock.com:** Diego Cervo (B). **36 Alamy Images:** TongRo Image Stock (1). **Getty Images:** Marc Romanelli (3). **Photolibrary.com:** Jim Toomey / age fotostock (4). **SuperStock:** Tetra Images (5); Stockbroker (2). **39 Alamy Images:** Nikreates (B). **40 Fotolia.com:** Theresa Martinez (b); Sean Gladwell (B); Ljupco Smokovski (D); Ekaterina Dushenina (C); Antonio Herrera (F). **Shutterstock.com:** Perry Correll (E); Miao Liao (A). **42 Alamy Images:** Janine Wiedel Photolibrary (tr); FirstShot (F); Cris Haigh (tl). **Fotolia.com:** Monkey Business (D); gunnar3000 (E). **Getty Images:** Maja Smend (B). **Pearson Education Ltd:** Tudor Photography (A). **Shutterstock.com:** Valentyn Volkov (C). **44 Shutterstock.com:** Barry Barnes (1 to 6, A to H). **45 Alamy Images:** moodboard (B). **Shutterstock.com:** Mares Lucian (E); Marek Pawluczuk (C); Baloncici (A); Alberto Tirado (D). **47 Shutterstock.com:** Artzzz. **48 Shutterstock.com:** Lisa F. Young. **49 Alamy Images:** studiomode (I); Isaac Iken Emokpae (E). **DK Images:** Gary Ombler (D). **Fotolia.com:** Ruben Pinto (F); design56 (B); aris sanjaya (C). **Pearson Education Ltd:** Tudor Photography (G). **Shutterstock.com:** photomak (H); Brian Tan (A). **50 DK Images:** Steve Gorton (l/Mixed); Steve Gorton (Gypsum); Matthew Ward (r/Mixed). **Fotolia.com:** Gudellaphoto (Inert); Andres Rodriguez (Box); Alex White (Hazardous). **Shutterstock.com:** stocksnapp (Wood); Ramona Heim (metal); Baloncici (glass); ARENA Creative (Biohazard). **51 Shutterstock.com:** Barry Barnes (1 to 4, 5 to 8). **52 Alamy Images:** Andres. **54 Shutterstock.com:** Lev Kropotov. **55 Shutterstock.com:** Zurijeta (t); punksid (b). **65 Alamy Images:** JTB Photo Communications, Inc. (r). **Getty Images:** © 2008 ChinaFotoPress (l). **Photoshot Holdings Limited:** De Agostini / World Illustrated (c). **70 Rex Features**.

Cover photo: *Front*: **Getty Images**: Driendl Group l; **Photolibrary.com**: Corbis / Bridge background, Corbis Premium RF r, UpperCut Images c

All other images © Pearson Education

Every effort has been made to trace the copyright holders and we apologise in advance for any unintentional omissions. We would be pleased to insert the appropriate acknowledgement in any subsequent edition of this publication.